"*Mirrors & Scales*"

&

My Pink Suit

by
Laura van der Meulen-Clark

This book is a work of fiction. Places, events, and situations in this story are purely fictional. Any resemblance to actual persons, living or dead, is coincidental.

ISBN: 1-4107-0050-X (e-book)
ISBN: 1-4107-0051-8 (Paperback)

This book is printed on acid free paper.

1stBooks - rev. 04/14/03

♥

For my precious son, Craig,
For my wonderful daughter, Laila
&
For my best Friend

♥

Holland, Friday morning, April 1st:

My name is Darra. Darra van Zandt: wife, mother, cook, cleaner, television watcher. I am a forty-seven year old American citizen living in Holland to be with (finally!) my *true* Soul Mate, a cute—yet, come to find out—fork-tongued blonde Dutchman. Part of this Dutchboy's pitch to move me to his country was not just the tease of delicious cheese and chocolate. No. I was more deceitfully lured by the myth that rain and moisture would keep my skin forever youthful; that bicycling—the most common mode of transportation, would make my thighs firm, my butt taut, and that learning his guttural language would surely improve my international marketability should I decide to return to the workforce one day. Seven years ago I was gullible enough to believe all that, what with me *finally* finding my "Soul Mate" and all, but these days his work takes him traveling around the world and I have become increasingly disenchanted with this peaceful lifestyle I so desperately prayed for.

Note to self: Be careful what you pray for.

1

We live in a conservative small village called Bozum, a bedroom community just outside of Amsterdam. My dad pronounces it *Booozum*, as in breasts. A very desirable, rather yuppie area to live in, Bozum is graced with huge white villas and ivy covered stone mansions filled with prosperous, yet unassuming tenants whose wealth is attained by scrapping plastic Blue Band Margarine cups completely clean, and saving guilders on automobile gasoline. It is not at all uncommon to cycle along side of a dignified looking woman in a $600 Max Mara suit, skillfully pedaling home with saddlebags filled from the butcher, baker, cheese, vegetable and wine shops—all the while single handedly controlling an umbrella to protect her *coiffure* from the rain.

Our home in Bozum is a dubbel-villa—well, not quite a villa—half a house really. Americans would call it a duplex. It was built in 1898 and has lots of character as well as flaws, like itty-bitty closets and one miniscule bathroom. Still, it is my home until I can go back to my real home, America. I try to keep it cozy for my six year old daughter, Christina, and for "Soul Mate" as well—when he's in town.

Today is April Fool's Day. I'm feeling appropriately foolish since I just caught myself pressing down on the bathroom window sill with two fingers as I stepped up on the scale for my daily weigh-in. This is a trick I use to get a lighter reading from the mean ol' *Health-o-Meter* when I can't handle the truth. I'm butt naked except for the rimless featherlite glasses necessary to read the meter—no rings, bracelets, necklaces or watches allowed, and, of course, I have just recently relieved myself of all bodily fluids. 146!—why, that's my post pregnancy weight after delivering Christina! I'm in big trouble I say to no one at all and hop off before releasing my fingertips from the ledge. The shot of my dimpled buttocks in the long mirror behind the bathroom door doesn't help. I make a mental note to rip the bugger off the door as soon as I get dressed, but that would have to be later I mumble as I head back to my warm bed with a couple of thinly peanut buttered *Wasa* crackers and a fresh cup of coffee. I clicked on the television just as today's episode of *As The World Turns* was about to begin...

2

Lucinda, the token "itch-bay" of my favorite soap, is confronting her pregnant adopted daughter, Lily, about the paternity of the adopted infant son of her birth mother, Iva, who is Lily's husband's brother, Holden—the child having been conceived during a drunken tryst with Julie, the token town whore, on the night before he married Lily, who wasn't aware of her own paternity until she was fifteen, when it was painfully revealed that she was really the daughter of Iva, who also conceived Lily under less than romantic conditions—date raped by the stable boy, Josh, when she, herself, was just fifteen.

Lucinda is hands down my favorite character. The last episode found her concocting some new wicked scheme to do what she does best— screwing up other people's lives, including her own and looking really glam through every crisis.

After the mother/daughter confrontation, Lucinda barks at Matthew, her man servant, to ready her jet to fly her right away to Switzerland so she can personally, and with great pleasure, give the ax to the doomed director of her European subsidiary in Zurich.

At least Lucinda is living an exciting life—as opposed to I am not. She's always throwing around those little French sayings like *fait accompli, coup d'état, vis-à-vis, cause célèbre.* She has people around her so intimidated that even when they don't really know what the hell she means, they just smile in agreement or frown in disapproval, whatever fits. God, I love that Lucinda. She's got girl cojones.

After ATWT, I brushed the cracker crumbs off my side of the bed, fluffed the white eyelet duvet in the air, and allowed it to float down to land any which way it wanted. I got dressed for the day but not before experiencing another frightening sight in the door mirror that I had forgotten to remove before my shower.

This week I am trying a new product called the *Sleek Patch*, a transdermal metabolism boosting skin patch. "A revolutionary breakthrough in weight loss technology" the package said. Each patch contains five milligrams of Fucus Vesiculosus extract, a seaweedy kind of fungi that clings to a rock formation off the coast of Scotland. This patch, "applied daily to a hairless"—and get this—'non-fatty' area, increases your normal body metabolism, melting away fat and pounds effortlessly." *Hel-looo?* If I *had* a 'non-fatty' area I surely would not find it necessary to go around with a perpetual band-aid trying to explain my "ow-ey" to inquisitive little kids.

I applied a new patch to my ankle bone. Owey.

"Darra," I said to myself in the long, much more flattering oval mirror above my cluttered dressing table, *"you are some kind of nut."*

Mirrors & Scales…The story of my life.

Downstairs I cleared away the breakfast dishes, tidied up the kitchen then checked the fridge for dinner fixins' for tonight. There was a small chicken breast but not enough for two, some leftover Uncle Ben's and a handful of limp green beans I had picked up from the vegetable shop four days ago.

Christina would be out of school at three o'clock. I had time to clean out the shed and hit the butcher, baker, vegetable and cheese shops before dashing into the school yard at 2:59. After living in Holland for seven years, I'm embarrassed to say that my Dutch still stinks. Therefore, I am on a precise schedule to arrive at the Koepelschool the moment the bell rings so I won't be pressed into chatting with one or more of the other chitchatting mothers hanging out on their bicycles. The mere thought of waving *"Daaag"* or worse—to be forced into a short Dutch conversation, gives me angst so I usually grab my kid and cycle off like I'm late for an appointment. Invariably, within minutes I am overtaken on the street because, after all, I've only been using a bike as my primary means of transportation for seven years while the Dutch have the advantage of being born with a bicycle seat already installed between their legs. Most moms ride away from school, and later pass me up, with one kid in front holding the umbrella, another in the back balancing a sack of groceries, and sometimes a baby is strapped to a chest.

Just thinking about this afternoon's school pick up gave me heart flutters. I guess it could also be a side effect of the *Sleek Patch*. The contraindications warning page did happen to mention that patches were not to be worn by heart patients. On the other hand, my goal is total sleekness. So I left it on.

I was working on dismantling the distorted bathroom door mirror when the phone rang.

"Met Darra." Dutch people always answer the phone with their name.

Daag Darra, here is Marielle. How is it with everything with you?

Marielle is my ever-ready baby-sitter. At twenty-two, she stills lives at home with her parents. Since she has been saving desperately for a flat of her own, she always seems to be available to sit these days.

Oh, hi there Marielle. Oh, we're fine, thanks. I'm just having a down day today. Is it still raining? It was coming down on the way back from school this morning. The saddlebags on my bike started to fill up and I had to stop on the Meijerkamplaan to turn them over before I could continue home.

Well, it is still raining now but don't worry, it looks like it might clear up before you have to go back to the school this afternoon. Anyway, I was wondering if it was possible that you are needing me to mind little Christina over the weekend? My parents are going to London for two nights and I can also go or I can also work for you?

Oh, that's awfully nice of you to check but no, hon, I really don't think I'll need you. Christina and I are just gonna stay close to home this weekend. But thanks for calling first. You have a great time, okay?

Okay, but if you change your mind and decide to go shopping in Amsterdam or anywhere else, I'll be here until half eleven. I hope to hear from you in fact, Darra. I very much enjoy being with little Christina. I like very much practicing my English with her.

I know you do, Marielle. I might need you next week but not this weekend. I'll call you, okay?

Okay. Kisses to Christina. Daaag.

Daaag, I repeated as I replaced the receiver on the cradle.

The rain was pelting down. Not a good day to work on our leaky shed. I lugged my sewing remnant basket into the *serre*, my "sun" room, to find some scraps to make Christina a jungle costume for a Lion King party next week. My tendency to be a pack rat was rewarded when I remembered that I had a leopard print T-shirt stuffed in a corner of an upstairs closet—a perfect body for the costume. Hah! And to think I was about to toss out the shirt just because I'm not the jungle animal print type. The last time I wore it was at least a year ago. That was the day I was pedaling to meet Christina at school and caught a glimpse of myself in the window of our local bakery as I rode through the center of town. My immediate impression was *Hey! Look at the hooker on a bicycle on her way to meet her John*—in Holland it would be meeting her *Jan*—and that was it. Never again. However, proving once again that one man's junk is another man's treasure, which is the unofficial flea market shopper's motto, I was finally able to put the print to good use. Fortunately, the jumbo size shoulder pads were covered in the same leopard print, so I pulled them out, folded them over to make some very puffy pointed ears and glue gunned them to a black velvet headband.

Ripping out those pads was a long time coming triumph. Not because of my ingenious use of an old T-shirt. No, it was something deeper. Last year, while visiting my family in California, I joined P.A.D.S., (**P**eople **A**gainst **D**roopy **S**houlders), a 12 Step Shoulder Pad Addiction Support Group, and since then I can proudly say that I have been able to taper myself down to just those flimsy little lifts that you can't really notice. Okay, I do have the occasional setback, but I'm taking One Day At A Time and feel that my recovery will be complete in about ten years, probably when pads are "in" again.

The therapeutic leopard outfit project took about eight minutes. I was cranky and bored out of my gourd, and no, I didn't have PMS. I get this feeling everyday but usually keep it to myself. It is only occasionally, say, once a month that I am uncontrollably compelled to share a few frustrations with my loved ones. Heh, heh.

The phone rang again as I was filing away my bag of fabric pieces.

Met Darra.

Hi Dar. Met Bineke. How is it? My Dutch sister-in-law.

Oh hi, Bini. Good. Good I guess. Just a little weather worn out. I was hoping for an early Spring. The darkness is really getting to me this year. It seems to get worse every year.

But why is that so, Darra? We, Ruud and me, we like to take long bicycle rides in the rain. Lekker. Or a long walk in the woods. Heerlijk! The wind and rain in our face. It is so natural. We love it very much. Why you do not do so also on such a beautiful day of rain? We love it!

Well, sorry, I don't. I'm a fair weather bike rider Bini, you know that. I don't think another seven years in this country is going to change me. I'm from Southern California. We only know one weather— perfect. Five minutes of sunshine out of twenty four hours does not make a nice day. Y'all are just so optimistic.

My, you are not lucky today are you? She always confuses "lucky" with "happy". *Why do you not light some nice moei candles around your house as Ruud and I do so we can be cozy together. Gezellig!*

I would but I don't have anyone here to be cozy with. Christina is not home until 3 o'clock.

And my brudder? He is still in Amerika? When is he back?

Yeah, he's still away. Maybe next week. I don't know, Bini. I said with an edge of annoyance I hoped she didn't detect. *Anyway, I'm sorry to have to hang up now but I was just about to go into town to pick up some things for dinner,* I lied. *I'll call you tonight, okay?* I lied.

We rang off agreeing to speak again tonight. I plopped down in my favorite chair, a pale yellow corduroy wing back facing the street, to

watch a northerly sheet of rain clean my *serre* windows for free. I lit a
tea light and placed it in the pumpkin shaped silver candle holder on
the table next to my chair. With the mood set, I reached for the
Moroccan patchwork pillow I brought home from the Clingincourt
flea market on my last trip to Paris. I cradled it to my chest and
pretended to be cozy. I felt dumb and restless and soon found myself
scrutinizing the cushion's handiwork with my fingertips. I wondered
who might belong to the pair of old leather skinned hands that sewed
the 43 twinkling dime sized mirrors into the rudimentary pattern. The
red, purple, green, black and orange threads woven into triangles,
ovals, squares and rectangles held my interest for five more minutes
until my thoughts fell once again on the mood I couldn't seem to
shake…

The day had started out normal. Christina, my blond, blue eyed
princess, woke me with a peck of kisses all over my face, as she does
every morning. Then we cuddled and told each other how much we
loved each other more than the other one did—a ritual I cherish
because it will soon be just a sweet memory once puberty kicks in.
While she dressed herself in her favorite purple and pink daisy granny
dress, I packed her lunch and peanut buttered her toast to eat on the
ride to school. With her pudgy six year old arms clinging to me on the
back of my bike, we sang "Oh What A Beautiful Morning"—it was
drizzling—down the tree lined cobblestone street for three blocks
until we reached the two story red brick school building.

More hugs and a dramatic send off:

Ik hou van jou Mama.
I love you too, sweetie poo.
No me more.
No me more.
No meeee.
No meeeeee…then she cheerfully skipped over to her friends proudly
swinging her new, pink Hello Kitty rugzak.

On the rainy ride back home I found myself recapping my life since
moving to Holland to marry my Soul Mate. I left Southern California
and a mediocre part-time career as a private investigator with high

hopes of living an idyllic, peaceful existence in another land even though they speak a strange tongue and ride more bicycles than drive cars. But the novelty quickly wore off. Daily language problems and a few mishaps on my bicycle put the kibosh on the dream soon enough so here I was, forty seven years old, years fleeting by, with no *raison d'etre*, as they say. And that was it. Nothing out of the ordinary today. My comfy yellow wing back would be my friend for the day I decided. I'll sit here all day and reflect on my life for the 91st time this year. It would not be the first time I spent the day in a chair. The sky darkened. The rain came down harder. I lit two more tea lights. It was ten past nine in the morning. Today, April Fool's Day, I felt totally different. I was ripe. The malaise that routinely dominates my daily life was replaced with a wicked little voice teasing me, cajoling me, challenging me to find that *raison d'être*—that "reason to be" and to quit my damn whining about it. I knew that if I didn't show some mature restraint, remembering my motherly and wifely responsibilities, I could easily be led astray by my first fantasy. I calmly glanced down at my watch. It was 9:15. Christina was in school. Soul Mate was in Texas, U.S.A. If I hurried I could catch the 9:45 train to Amsterdam and relax on a closed-in terrace, have a coffee and an appeltart and try to ignore the feeling. Yeah, that sounds good.

Or, if I really hustled, I could make the 9:33 Eurocity to Paris, the "Etoile du Nord".

Paris. Just getting on the train would be escape enough. When we arrive in Brussels and the dining car is attached, I could finagle a single seat in the First Class dining car and nurse a small, yet ridiculously expensive plate of assorted cheeses and half a bottle of the *vin du trein* for three hours until we reached Gare du Nord.

So, foolish me on this apropos date, I opted for the *OR*. Yeah, foolish or not, I felt better already.

I quickly dialed up Marielle hoping to reach her before she was off for the weekend.

Hi Marielle. It's me, Darra. I'm so glad to still find you at home, hon.

Darra! Is there something? I was just packing a few things for London. My parents, they are lucky for me to go with them, so I said I yes.

Oh, Marielle. That's what I wanted to talk to you about. You see... and then a splendidly clever lie just rolled off my tongue:

My uncle, ummm Walter, that's right, my Uncle Walter just phoned from Paris, having just arrived with my dying aunt, Aunt ummm Trudy. Yeah, Uncle Walter and Auntie Trudy. My beloved godparents. Auntie Trudy had been flown in to receive last hope treatment at a famous-I-made-up-some-name-of-a-French-hospital, and as I was her favorite niece and godchild, would it be possible for me to go there as soon as possible to spend at least one day with her. In fact, it may even be her last day. That's what the doctor said anyway. I added a little choke sound as my sentence trailed off. One day, that's all. She wouldn't last the night. Choke.

How very sad, Darra. Of course. I am ever too happy to stay with Christina, you know that from me. I did not look so much forward to the weekend with my parents anyway, she whispered into the mouthpiece.

Funny, I knew Marielle didn't believe my cock-a-mamie story one little bit, but I didn't give a fig. She needed the money. I had to get away. We both win. She agreed to pick up Christina promptly from school, feed and bathe her, read to her, tuck her in and reassure her that Mama would be home in time for Barbie & Ken's wedding tomorrow. God knows I try but I am simply not a mom who enjoys buttoning buttons the size of apple seeds on Ballroom Barbie's white *peau de soie* wedding gown, or squeezing a teeny pleated tuxedo shirt over Ken's half inch biceps. However, as maid of honor I do have that obligation and will most certainly be there in time, I promised.

That would be great, Marielle. I'll call to talk to Christina when I get to my hotel, okay?

But of course, Darra. Do not worry about us. We will be fine. Daag now.

10

My faithful travelin' outfit is a comfy oversized soft gray corduroy boat neck dress. I keep it travel ready at the back of my closet along with a quilted flower print duffel bag containing a matching cosmetic bag and two pairs of underwear. I slipped the dress over my head careful not to muss my make-up or my do, buffed my black flats with a dab of Vaseline and a wad of toilet paper and twirled around the room.

I was sure my *raison d'etre* was just around the corner.

Paris, Friday afternoon

T he "Etoile du Nord" pulled into Gare du Nord at 2:20 PM right on schedule. I had joined the First Class dining car in Brussels, enjoyed the half bottle of *L'Authentique* red table wine but found the skimpy assorted cheese board didn't fill me up. Within a half an hour the métro from the train station dropped me at St-Germain des Prés where I scored a coveted table on the sidewalk at *Café Aux Deux Magots*. I ordered a glass of *du vin rouge* and a *Croque Monsieur* while I waited for my life to take a turn.

Come on. Turn.

It's hard to describe the rush of arriving in a big city alone. If I want to walk for hours I can. I can sit and get sloshed if I want. And, yes, I can even smoke cigarettes while getting sloshed if I so desire. I can eat a whole baguette stuffed with a pound of greasy salami and some of that French cheese that smells like stinky feet—if I want to. I can go where I want to when I want to. I don't have to deal with "if you go with me here, I'll go with you there" mentality of the Bobsie Twins School of Travel. I just happen to enjoy traveling solo. I've even been told that relishing one's own company is a sign of good mental health. Why is that, I wondered. Why am I not a good sharer of experiences?

Just as I was about to become maudlin in the City of Light, my minuscule table *pour une* was almost toppled over by a frantic fortysomething-ish blond woman who looked as if she was in desperate need of a fast taxi. She turned quickly to steady my table then continued her flight out of the café but not before I got a better look at her face.

I looked at my reflection in my café neighbor's silver-plated teapot and saw myself for the second time in as many seconds.

Where was I going? And in such a hurry?

I closed my eyes tight and took a humongous gulp of wine. I raised my face up to the new, warm April sun, flashed a thought about Christina and how I should be picking her up from her little school at this very moment. She'd hop on the back of my bike and we'd sing our favorite after school song, Sade's *Kiss of Life* as we pedaled into town for a Coke date…

Instead I was in Paris. On boulevard St-Germain. In a café. And afraid to open my eyes.

Pardonnez-moi, mademoiselle. Est-ce que cette table est occupée?

Lone traveler at 12 o'clock, I guessed before looking straight up into the sun and the eyes of the stranger. He leaned over my table to block the glare but in the process got recklessly close to my face. Real close. My forty-seven year old face is attractive only under certain lighting conditions and bright sunlight is not one of them.

What? I mean, ex-cus-io-me-o, what did you say?…I don't par-lay Fran-cez mucho, replied Darra the Dorkalette. Did I just say *ex-cus-io-me-o? Mucho?* Seems I had just created a new hybrid language combining Italian, French, Spanish, and the easiest of all languages to master—English.

The golden hair on his forearms glistened in the sun, giving off a sexy kind of glow, if such a thing is possible. Tall and enviably slender, he was dressed casually in an outfit that I'm sure cost beaucoup bucks— short sleeved moss green silk shirt, "aubergine" slacks and a thin brown alligator belt with a pewter buckle carrying what looked like a logo of some fancy schmancy designer. His belt had about six buckle holes, but he had the kind of body that would have no problem living with a one hole belt if indeed only one hole was provided. This guy never had a puffy day in his life. His soft cordovan loafers looked new, the leather soles probably still slippery as they made their first hard surface contact today. His cobalt blue eyes were begging permission to take me back to his suite at the *Hôtel Prince de Galles*, but poor chap, his mind took over his heart. Instead—his mouth, surrounded by full, smooth rosy lips embracing a perfect set of gleaming white teeth, uttered in T H E most adorable broken accent: *Iz ziz table free?*

Free? I wanted to say. I don't know about the table, but *I* am. It was a lie of course. Soul Mate was waiting for me—well maybe not in the physical sense of the word, but in a dutiful, commitment sort of waiting way in Holland. That would be all fine and good if he spent more time in Holland and less time following his professional goals. But mostly it's just Christina and me. When we aren't playing Barbies, my daily thrill consists of vacuuming and peeling mounds of potatoes, the staple food of The Netherlands.

Oh, oui, no probl-em-o. Prob-lem-O? Did I say that? There I go with my new language again.

I sucked in my gut, stretched my neck up as high as it would go to cancel out part of the double chin God gave me as a gag gift on my 45th birthday. I wondered if I could still pass for thirty-five. A mature thirty-five would be good.

He ordered an espresso and sure enough, just as I took *way* too big of a bite from my sandwich, I sensed a brief but meaningful glance headed my way. Our tables were touching each other. I couldn't help wishing I hadn't rushed out of the house this morning without

14

checking the ol' chin for superfluous hairs. Yet another gift from my best friend, God, the Humorist.

Jacques—that's the made up name I gave him—drank his espresso with style. You know, long slim manicured fingertips barely holding the toy size cup handle. And I think he was wearing Armani parfum, to match his pants.

Not wanting to torment either one of us any longer, I made the first move to leave. Besides, I didn't have a hotel for the night and it was getting close to five o'clock. After dropping sixty francs on the table I stood up and as gracefully as poss, made my way through the maze of other touching table tops until I reached the sidewalk along boulevard St. Germain. I turned around to leave Jacques with a wanton gaze, but he too, obviously not wanting to start something we both knew we couldn't finish, split.

After a subtle survey in both directions for this suddenly gone stranger, I turned left out of *Aux Deux Magots* and headed toward Place St-Michel, about ten minutes walking. I was beginning to feel it. Alive, that is. I sneaked looks at my reflection in every shop window, noticing that despite the burden of the flower print duffel bag on my right shoulder, I had a spry lilt to my walk. My back was erect. If I could have seen my eyes, they probably had a twinkle in them.

I ended up at the same seedy hotel I usually stay in when I am unexpectedly in Paris. It's on the Left Bank in the Latin Quartier near Place St-Michel. The *Grand Hôtel Royale*. Well, it isn't Grand and it isn't Royale. It's a flea bag is what it is, but they always have a single without shower or toilet for the equivalent of about forty U.S. bucks. It works for me. It would be nice if I could say that the staff were the reason why I always return. No. Every time I show up they act as if they've never seen me before, and for that matter, couldn't care less if they ever see me again. Not only that, they make sure I am aware that they are doing me a great favor by allowing me to pay them to sleep in one of their cubicles.

The focal point of the offensively appointed lobby is Marcel, the friendly proprietor. He was reclining on a black fur sofa behind the reception desk slurping an espresso in a fashion very unlike Jacques' elegant manner of espresso drinking. I watched in awe at his attempt at a last drag from a half inch long *Gitane*. He had an unhealthy head of hair that looked like an accumulation of pubes collected from around all of the toilets in what I just decided was the dumpiest and most unfriendly hotel in Paris. The bushy unibrow dashing across the width of his pocked marked face wiggled frantically as he read from a worn pocketbook. I *ahemed* twice before he could bring himself to acknowledge my presence. Expected. While he took his time coming up with a vacant *chambre* in my price range, I took a look around.

Oh man. The same two ca-ca brown wing back chairs facing each other in the reception area. From a distance they didn't look all that bad but up close one could see that the shabby tweed upholstery had many ways to hide its age and imperfections. Perhaps only a repeat guest would be wise to their tricks and I, being one of them, happen to know for a fact that the avocado, brown and orange Afghan draped casually over the right arm was there solely to hide the fact there *was* no real right arm. The stuffing had been pulled out, probably by a mean old cat, and replaced with a throw pillow which had been folded over and secured with a couple of half inch thick rubber bands. The other chair had sprung a spring, so a thirty pound orange and white calico named Madeleine—looking mean and a bit long in the tooth, stretched belly up and spread eagle across the seat cushion, her paws and claws poised to attack anyone attempting to sit down. A round brass and glass coffee table with crusty glass ring stains around its entire circumference separated the chairs and covered most of a very large animal stain on the gold shag carpet. Four chrome wall sconces with way too high wattage lined the white brick foyer wall leading into this, le *Grand Royale* Flea bag.

I reluctantly paid Marcel the new room rate which had skyrocketed to over sixty dollars, accepted the key which was attached to a log the size of a breadboard—intentionally oversized so guests would think twice before deciding to take it with them as they walked the streets of Paris, and proceeded up the three flights of stairs to my assigned cubicle.

After a shampoo and a long overdue leg shave in a shower stall designed to cater to whatever Pygmy tourist trade might come through the city, I laid flat on the bed to work on zipping up my size 12 black *Levi's*. Once I got the bulk of my tummy safely confined, I looked pounds lighter. I think the Sleek Patch on my ankle was working as well. I threw on a white 100% cotton blouse and daringly tucked it "in". Uh Uh. No can do. I quickly yanked it out so as not to give it that tell tale waist wrinkle and topped it off with a coordinating trendy gold and brown paisley vest. As the *pièce de résistance* I generously spritzed Eternity on all of my pulse points.

I must say, the grimy mirror in my 4x4 room was somewhat more forgiving than the one I planned to trash when I got home. I saw a real person in the glass, albeit an uncomfortable one. Although I felt like a stuffed Polish kielbasa, I looked damned good. I recently had an excellent blond hair weave done by my new hairdresser, Farideh, a Persian version of Ivana Trump: mountains of blond hair, lotsa foundation, blue eye shadow and red lipstick that she swears she applies only once in the morning, *Dahhlink*. Right.

My hazel green eyes looked alive for the first time in a long time and save for the wretched neck and chin area, I did not have too many wrinkles for my age. I hate that. For my age. Just how many wrinkles should I have for my age, anyway? 23? 2023? What?

Misty Mink brown pencil filled in my sparse brows. The eyebrows were not a gift from God, but a self inflicted error in judgment left over from the 60's when pencil thin brows were cool. Nobody bothered to tell me before I shaved them that they wouldn't grow back or that one day nonstop Brooke Shields brushes would be a look to die for. I colored my lips with Rum Raisin, a choice my Color Me Beautiful advisor insists is a definite no-no, dotted the mole above my upper lip, a la Cindy Crawford, and concluded that I was as good as I was gonna get.

I felt pretty darn cute and surprisingly confident, especially after performing my personal pump-me-up mantra in front of the complimentary mirror:

Mah name is Darra,
I'm Number ONE,
Mah rep-u-tay-shun has just begun....
If ya see me comin' bettah step aside...
Cuzthislitt'lchick don't take no jive,
Uh huh.
Ole' Ole' uh huh.
Ole' Ole' uh huh.

I had only been away from home for seven hours but I felt wonderfully different already. The shock of seeing a dead ringer for me at *Café Aux Deux Magots* and my harmless flirtation with the elusive Jacques right after that could have something to do with jazzing up my day.

I felt a bit feisty. I opened the bottle of cheap red I brought from home with a BIC pen that I always keep for such an emergency. It's a handy trick picked up from a girlfriend who travels a lot and likes to drink wine in her hotel room at night. Even though I left the house in a hurry, I also remembered to bring a real wine glass along. Maybe I *am* a bit nutso after all...

After a glass of wine and a nibble of stink foot cheese picked up at the Greek deli next to the hotel, I went downstairs to phone Marielle. Marcel was also dabbling in the *du vin* and a package of *Cheezy Doodles*. He was still engrossed in the dog eared pocketbook. He didn't notice me or my fresh fragrance at the counter until I cleared my throat twice and said, *Bunjur, Mar-cel, como tally voo?* He raised his pubic head, killed his cigarette with an experienced brown thumbnail, took my request to call Holland and promptly went back to his read, "How to Be #1 In The Competitive Hospitality Industry". Just kidding. I couldn't make out the title but it had a picture of two creatures—one female human and one hairy and steamy looking bovine doing "it". Before I could check it out for details, my call home to Bozum came through.

Met Christina—mij moeder is niet thuis, my bilingual princess sang into the receiver.

Hello, sweetie poo-poo. That's what I call her sometimes. She loves it. *How are you, my precious girl?*

Where are you, Mama? Mama, Mama, today I was in gym and you know what, Mama? You know what? Jan Pieter tried to kiss me and I told him not to do it and he did anyway and the Juf didn't even do anything to him. Will you tell him not to do it again, Mama?

Here we go. Guilt trip.

Of course I'm gonna tell him he better not ever do that again and don't worry, I'll give him one of my looks that'll make him not do it ever again, okay, Poops?

Okay, Mama. Wanna talk to Marielle? Bye. The receiver fell to the floor.

All was fine on the home front so I pushed my luck and dangled the pecuniary carrot one notch closer by asking Marielle if she could possibly stay one more night as Auntie Trudy was starting to rally and she wanted to discuss the revisions of her Will with her favorite niece—me. Heh. Heh. I told Marielle I would make it worth her while and she hung up already making plans for the upcoming move into her own flat.

Marcel collected fifty francs for the call. He gave me an ever so slight hint of a grin exposing a grand total of six green teeth complete with nicotine and *Cheezy Doodle* highlights. Perhaps I should have welcomed the new recognition I justly deserved as a repeat guest, but judging from his reading material and the bulge in his black *Levi's* that I guessed was not a kielbasa, I would have preferred that he regarded me as the same non-entity of past visits. I was definitely not into a Last Tango In Paris with this grease ball.

Out on the street I breathed deeply, walked as if I had a direction and wondered if I'd be able to sleep in that hotel with Marcel in charge of the room keys.

19

In ten minutes I was in my favorite part of the Left Bank. Away from the ethnic Greek, North African and Italian restaurants and food stands in Place St-Michel, real French cafés and restaurants dot narrow, cobblestone streets around the university area. I decided on *Le Petite Chât,* a restaurant I've been to many times. I am a creature of habit. Same-old. Same-old. The food is okay. The service is sort of okay. It's cheap. I ordered what I always order: salad, *omelette au fromage* and lotsa, lotsa bread. And of course, a demi-carafé of the *vin du table.*

Same-old. Same-old.

My dinner itself was mediocre, as usual. After I scraped my plate with an end of my baguette like the French people do, I got down to the real reason I was there. For some odd reason, I think this place has a reputation for attracting misfits of all sorts—present company excluded—so I spend most of my time observing my fellow diners, personalizing each one by giving them names and personal histories.

Sitting at a candle lit corner table across from me was Madame Bouchet, very possibly Brigitte Bardot's much older sister. She is a former sex kitten still rejecting that persistent overdue invitation to Old Ladydom. She keeps plugging away at it but it's obviously getting increasingly more difficult, so lately she's using less energy to get the same results. Or so she thinks. The exhilarating high she used to get when she looked into a mirror is now replaced with a disappointing sigh. It looks as if a jealous bitch friend gave her some ill advice about how to age gracefully—that advice being that MORE of everything would certainly counteract the ravages of Old Ladydom. So, what we've got now is more make-up foundation filling in the deepening cracks that no longer can be referred to as laugh lines, unless it's in jest, of course. Mascara, on what's left of her eyelashes––no doubt once her selling feature—is tarred on so thick that her walnut shell lids are drooping by the weight of it all. The artificial lip line is borrowed back from the days when it used to be there. It is painted into a permanent pout position readily on call to say *"oui"* should an offer come by. Any offer. And finally, the fire engine red rat's nest on her head was, I suppose, just a humorous go at pretending to have abandonly tossed it on top of her head to turn out this package *au naturel.* Bless her heart.

The saddest part of all is that while she was depending on the candlelight to soften this "wholesome" look, it just wasn't happening, hon. Now, ideally, candles are a senior lady's best friend, but tonight, because of the unwise seating angle she chose, the light danced and flickered across her face forming an animated, and sorry to say, "What Ever Happened to Baby Jane" mask. I blessed her heart again.

I moved on to the dining companion—her son, Jean-Pierre:

Jean-Pierre was the exact opposite description of mom. Everything spanking new. He had a twenty-four year old head of glossy chocolate curls, a few of which were strategically placed to accent his pale post pubescent face. His deep violet eyes surrounded by top and bottom bottle brush lashes, obviously inherited from his mother, had an exciting devilish sparkle to them, probably also hereditary. Pillowy lips—Mick Jagger lips—quivered sexily as he breathed through a prominent Greek nose, nostrils flaring ever so slightly with every inhalation.

I was amused to watch this young stallion dressed in black make eye contact with the beautiful Françoise who was sitting alone in the table in front of him and directly behind his mom. She looked even younger—maybe twenty-one, twenty-two. A flimsy yellow flowered dress rested smoothly on her rail thin body. There was what looked like a watercress and tomato sandwich on her plate and a half liter of Evian to wash it down. Her hair was chestnut and slicked back in what she would call easy but what I call quite daring if you have a fleshy neck—a tight ballerina bun. She had a petite nose, warm and sensuous dark eyes with those to die for thick brows, and her lips, well, her lips and mouth together covered at least a third of her face. Now *her* mouth was also in a permanent pout position, but I'm afraid on her it sent out a totally different signal than the pout put on by Jean-Pierre's mom. Oh yeah. It was positioned to say "*non,*" but then also "*oui,*" depending on just how much she felt like teasing a fella on any given day. I wasn't fooled by her demure façade, however. As soon as she was sure she had made contact with her curly headed victim, she tilted her head just *so*, then used those lips and mouth and tongue of hers to make a skillful, kinky kind of move with her baguette, which must have also moved the studly Jean-Pierre, if you catch my drift…

Ah, young love.
Ah, young.

The clump of black knitting wool at Madame Bouchet's feet moved so I named it Fifi. She gave one of those aggravating whining sounds that I took to be an prearranged command to her owner for attention or food or both. Seeming to know which was which, Madame obediently offered a sliver of the blood rare steak on her plate, and Fifi thanked her with a juicy finger lick. I am not an animal person, per se, so I silently yucked to express my disapproval and unconsciously wiped my hands off with my napkin.

While my eyes were still down in the vicinity of Madame Bouchet's shiny, red stiletto heels, I caught one finding its way up the black pant leg of Jean-Pierre, which meant I had to immediately switch gears on the mother and son thing.

As much as my heart went out for Madame Bouchet, the story line was becoming much more intriguing. I poured the remains of the carafe into my empty glass, took a swill, put a disinterested expression on my face and sat back to watch the rest of the show.

Tonight was to be the last evening with her young paramour. She was trying passionately to keep his attention. While he gazed dreamily over her red beehive, her failing eyesight and wishful thinking assumed the gaze was meant for her, so she went into her cigarette lovemaking performance. This woman could smoke a cigarette unlike any other woman except maybe Bette Davis. She didn't just take a drag, inhale and blow it out like most people. No, she made a production out of it.

Here's how it went: With eyes brimming with cognac that longed to drink up one sexy Jean-Pierre, Madame Bouchet deeply inhaled from a freshly lit Benson & Hedges, dipped her head down, then up again, stretching her weathered neck to its full length. When it was finally time to exhale, the thin trail of smoke made its way out of the pursed little "oui" opening, the head slowly descended, eyes rolled back through fluttering eyelids that ended up in a closed position. A demure, beckoning smile etched across her face. Sadly, all the while her eyes were closed, J.P. had faked a dropped napkin giving him permission to size up Françoise from a different angle and he missed the whole weird mating ritual performed especially for him.

The whole scene began to depress me to no end so I decided to leave. I paid the bill, pulled out my Cover Girl compact to check the mirror, sighed, and made my way to the exit.

The only other thrill so far for the evening was when the waiter, who I felt should have recognized me as a regular by now, did. It didn't improve the service. He just gave me one of those deadpan I-have-much-more-important-things-to-do-with-my-time-than-wait-on-you faces and, in English, mind you, said *"Ave a nize day"* as he gave me my change.

I must admit that in a pitiable sort of way, I felt pretty good about myself. I mean, I was three for three in the recognition department: first there was Jacques, (even though he disappeared on me), then Marcel and now the President of France moonlighting as a waiter. Must be my new bottle of Eternity that I have to confess I squirted on *way* beyond the major pulse points. I made a mental note to write a letter of customer satisfaction to Calvin Klein when I got home.

Rue Jacob was quiet even though it was only nine o' clock. I set out to walk off my dinner, softly singing *Kiss of Life,* but not loud enough for anyone to mistake me for a nut:

There must have been an angel by my si-de…
Something Heavenly led me to youuu.
…dum dee dummm. For-got the wo-rds….
You gave me, the Kiss of Life,
Kiss of Li-ife…

Oh yeah. Kiss of Life. That's what I needed. A Kiss of L.I.F.E.

Instead, my mind took a short trip to the uncomfortable Land of Guilt, starting with the way I up and left home after a two minute deliberation this morning. What about when Soul Mate calls from the States to see how his two girls were doing without him? This negative thought process was threatening to ruin my entire weekend and it probably would have had I not spotted the perfect café to enjoy an espresso with a Grand Marnier back and a cig.

Walking past Parisian sidewalk cafés where everyone is there just to watch/catch people make a walking mistake always worries me, so when my left foot misjudged the length of the planter in front of the table I had selected, I immediately twirled around and plopped into the nearest vacant chair. To convince the watchers that this was a planned seating decision, I quickly pulled out a piece of paper and with my trusty, versatile BIC—furrowed brow added for effect—I pretended to be capturing an important point for a meeting I had with Prime Minister Jacques Delors in the morning. I put the scribbled note back in my bag and smiled back at the watchers.

Speaking of Jacques, I imagined the other Jacques—my Jacques—to be somewhere in the city, possibly Maxim's, or its posh equivalent, probably just sitting down to a fashionably late supper with a slim, elegant French broad in a Little Black Dress.

Boy, was I ever wrong.

Three

My fran-cez had not improved since earlier in the afternoon, but it didn't turn out to be necessary. He judged the planter precisely, as one should, and took the rattan chair next to mine. He didn't ask to be invited. He just did it.

Bon soir…My name iz Jacques…

Whoa! The lone stranger returns. This time the dim evening lighting was in my favor.

Iz it not pozzible zhat we know each othzer from anothzer time, anothzer plaze?

I deduced that this guy didn't realize what a cornball approach this was, excusing it as his limited knowledge of a second language, but look who's talking:

No, I said. *I'm quite sure I would have remembered*—based on the totally hunkiness of your perfect face and bod. I didn't really say the hunkiness

25

part—just that I would have remembered, also a corny response. It was like we were having a cornball contest and so far we were tied for first place.

I finished my Grand Marnier, took a dramatic Madame Bouchet drag on my Marlboro red and snubbed it out as gracefully as possible.

Pulling up super close—so close that I could confirm my earlier deduction that he was wearing Armani cologne to match his outfit, Jacques eye-locked me and said in a soft, shy voice, *I know ziz iz, how you zay, very forward of me az we know each othzer five minutez only, mais, I 'ave zeez tick-ettes for ze Zteel Pulze at ze Elysee Montmartre and my zeester she iz for me not pozzible to alzo go. Iz it not pozzible zhat you go wiz me?*

"STEEL PULSE" Hmmm. Sounded like a new Schwarzenegger film. I deliberated the offer for two seconds. *Sure*, I said, *why not*, assuming I couldn't get into any mischief at some action movie for crying out loud. We wouldn't have to fight off the mutual urge for unbridled passion that we might otherwise be subjected to had he proposed one of those suggestive French nudie flicks. Besides he was going to take his sister…how cute.

Well where have *I* been? Steel Pulse was *not* a movie, but a hot reggae group recording live for their newest CD at the Elysee Montmartre that evening.

We inched our way through two beefy bouncers bastioned at the double doors to admit those of us with the right appearance. I sensed that perhaps I wouldn't get in on my own merit, but luckily Jacques qualified for both of us. We were ushered on in leaving a throng of unfortunates outside. The concert hall was just as squishy and at first unbearably claustrophobic, but soon the smell and heated sensation of a thousand sweaty bodies moving like *all ah we is one, mahn* to a throbbing island beat took over any rational thoughts of what a middle-aged, peri-menopausal housewife was doing in a place like this.

The pot also helped. I mean I got it second hand but I couldn't help inhaling, could I? The whole arena was engulfed with the stuff. What's a gal to do?

Luv me, luv me like dis ah.
Rub me, dub me like dat deh.
We got ah life to live-ah,
So let's make ah starht….

Ever notice how so many songs talk about "life" and "living" these days?

The music was so loud that we couldn't really talk to get to know each other, so we did what everyone else did—we *rubbed ah dubbed like dat deh*. It was more like sardines dancing in a tin filled with two too many fish in it, actually. Jacques was a perfect gentleman throughout the concert. I was sure that he intentionally restrained himself due to the fact that we had only just met and he didn't want to muck up any plans he had for the very near future. Like immediately after the show.

At 3:00 AM the last of the crowd still milling around the steps of the Elysee Montmartre thinned out to two—me and you-know-who. I was still intoxicated from the combination of pot and warm beer I had drunk during the most bizarre evening I had spent in the last seven years.

But I felt alive. And what I think they call "*irie*". Yeah, I felt irie.

We walked through the darkened streets of Montmartre, stopping only once to excuse myself to slip around the corner to barf. I only drank two beers, but I had a muddled, yet at the same time, very distinct feeling that any vital decision making would not be in the cards this evening. It was a strange sensation I was sure had to be caused by something more chemical than the effects of a few beers and a teensy bit of second hand reefer smoke.

Turns out I wasn't given an opportunity to make any decision—vital, stupid or otherwise.

Saturday morning

I woke up with that cotton mouth feeling I used to get in the sixties when I'd take diet pills to drop a few pounds The eternal weight watcher, me. This time the cotton was real. It was stuffed in so tight causing my upper lip—fake mole now surely rubbed away—to push up against my nostrils, which blocked what little air there seemed to be left in wherever I was being held captive. I feel so naked without my mole. My arms were drawn behind me, bound at the elbows with probably the same rope used for my ankles. Looked like shoelaces, but I couldn't be sure. One of my soft contact lens was gone and I could feel the other one stuck to my right cheek.

The room was dark but I could tell it was small and probably dirty with leftover cheese and dried up baguettes strewn haphazardly across the wooden floor.

Since moving to Holland, I have slowly been developing claustrophobia. It is presently in full blown stage. My own self analysis told me that perhaps it could be related to living in a tiny country with big people. As an example, one of the most commonly

28

used words in the Dutch language is *gezellig*. That means "cozy". What I call "small," Dutch people call "cozy". Most people in Holland live in small, *gezellig* houses. Small houses are sure to have small closets. A lot of people don't know this, but these small closets are actually alive. The clothes that appear to be just clothes folded and piled high on shelves, have a tendency to attack you when you try to leave the closet. Usually, when you turn around in one of these small rooms, you have an article that you had not planned to wear, on your head, or shoulder, or both. Small bathrooms naturally have small showers with plastic curtains that attack your butt. So, you see, Dutch shower stalls are also alive, just like Dutch closets. Cozy restaurants will have small groups of large Dutch people easing their way very sneakily in between you and a three inch space to try to take the small table you are reasonably sure you are next in line for. My American interpretation of "cozy" does not include any of the above. I could go on but even just thinking about it makes me have to grasp for breath—something I was not able to do in my current predicament. The feeling of confinement, even in the best case scenario, freaks me out, *sooooo*, as one can imagine, I was ready to explode. My heart was for sure palpitating this time and I don't think it was the Sleek Patch kicking in.

I was in **T**rouble.

Just as I finished a really sincere get-me-outta-here-and-I-promise-to-be-good prayer to my Pal in Heaven, my date from the previous evening entered the room. A shock of sunshine temporarily blinded my already handicapped eyes. I squinted to see if I could read his face. Since I was the one on the floor looking like a roped heifer and he was standing above me with perfect creases in his eggplant Armani slacks, his scuff less Ferragamo loafers still highly buffed enough that I could see myself in them—as well as noticing the gun he was twirling in his left hand—I surmised that he was not there to rescue me.

His cohort, Henri—probably Hank for short, reached down to pluck the cotton balls out of my mouth. I was thirsty.

29

Hank had what we Americans consider to be typical French features: small boned structure, close set eyes, full lips, prominent bony nose. Although the same description could also apply to oh, let's say, the late and very delicious François Truffaut,—the composition of Hank's physical characteristics was a minus one on a scale of ten. It's like all the components are there, they just got placed wrong, unlucky fella. His scoring might have improved considerably if he had washed the crud out of his murky dog doo hair and scalp and extricated the buzillion blackheads punctuating his face. *And* he would also have to ditch the Fu Manchu that didn't seem to be working.

I was right about the size of the room and it's substandard living condition. I was also right about the old cheese and bread. These guys obviously never heard of the universal "when in doubt, throw it out" rule.

I had not counted on the two hearty looking rodents I will hereinafter refer to as Steve and Pete.

Steve and Pete were too busy enjoying their *petit dejéuneur* to give me as much as a beady glance. I can't explain what happened the moment I spotted Steve and Pete, but it wasn't fear or disgust or repulsion as one would think. It was as if they were assigned to get me out of this mess. I was beginning to wonder if the effect of the Mickey that Jacques slipped into my beer was affecting my already overactive imagination. I say that because, and I know it sounds crazy, but all of a sudden Steve and Pete seem to take on individual personalities—Pete, the leader and Steve, the more laid back, roll with the punches type. One was even cuter than the other: Rat Steve.

I shot a prayer request to that Guy in the Sky with the Great Sense of Humor and swore that not only would I be a good girl, I would also tithe ten percent of my future earnings to the starving people in Africa or wherever He wanted to allocate it. Whatever. *You name it, You got it*, I vowed.

Jacques rattled off some French in my face, finger wagging. I could only catch *"ze paperz"* this and *"ze paperz"* that but not enough to understand the dilemma.

Say what? I said through parched lips. *I don't comprehend-o what you are saying to me. I am an Amer-i-can-o remember? We only speak English.* That's the unwritten law with Americans. We Americans believe the entire world should speak one language—that being the easiest to learn. That language is E N G L I S H, you pompous twerp.

I didn't really recite our American Language Law thing or mention the pompous part. I wanted to but the fuzz in my head was beginning to lift and I was able to make the clear decision not to rub this guy the wrong way. His once sumptuous drop dead blue eyes were no longer sumptuous but they did manage to maintain their drop dead expression.

If I had a free arm, now would be the time to bang my forehead and cry, *"I shoulda' hadda' V-8!"* It all fit in: My twin darts passed me in a busy café; a dashing yet obviously misled stranger follows me through the night until we meet again by "chance". Yeah, right. He spikes my beer when I was most vulnerable, blah, blah, blah.

Ze paperz, he screeched. *If you don't hand over ze paperz it will be pozzible zhat you will be dead in five minutez. We must 'ave shipment and paperz for Mabouk today! Maintenant! Now!*

Talk about your brainless idiot. Where in the world did he think I was going to plant *ze paperz* in these jeans? I was just this minute thinking that if I could have any wish in the world granted with no strings attached, it would be that Hank would unbutton the top two Genuine *Levi's* Brand studs to relieve the stress on my waistline. In fact, I was beginning to question my purchase decision with these damn jeans. I should've gone with the ones my seventy-five year old dad looks so cute in. The inside label boasts: "With Just a *Skoash* More for Comfort". Har, har, hardy har har. My dad doesn't need a skoash more. He has no longer has butt. I think God took it away from him at forty-five, just about the same age I received the chin thing.

Lookit, Jacques, I said. *This is a crazy mistake. I don't have a clue about what you want. I'm just a housewife who decided to take a break, that's all. You have me confused with someone else. Someone else has what you want. I don't. Please believe me. I have to catch the 11 o'clock train to Amsterdam so I can pick up my daughter from day camp today,* I lied...*otherwise she'll be alone and confused and won't know what to do. She's only six, Jacques. PUL-EEZZE let me go.*

I don't know if I was talking way too fast for him or if he could tell I was lying, but my pleading tactic failed. At least I was spared the butt of his gun, but the heavy duty love-tap he walloped across my still moving mouth told me that it was time to come up with Plan B.

Plan B?

Before I had a chance to coordinate this not yet created brilliant Plan B, there came a commotion from the next room. Another room? That's funny, I thought we were all alone in a cardboard box with no windows, no air, therefore no way to breathe, ultimately leaving us to die a slow and agonizing death through suffocation.

Hank jammed the soggy cotton puffs back down my throat then he and Loverboy quickly left the room. I took the opportunity to force myself to practice a relaxation and positive imaging exercise that I have used on various occasions for calming down or improving my self-image. And yes, for weight control.

I closed my eyes. Normally I would take three deep breaths to reach my Alpha level of consciousness, but under the circumstances I had to fast forward to the next step which was to relax every muscle in my body; to allow my body to go *com-plete-ly limp,* also no easy feat. Under these adverse conditions, I was only able to reduce my muscle tension level to that of a Genoa salami, but I was still able to find my quiet place.

My quiet place is along the banks of a slow moving river. I'm lying on a blanket under an old apple tree on a grassy knoll. I am reading a great book. I wrote the book. I'm wearing super short khaki shorts and a sleeveless white cotton midriff blouse. I am not wearing a bra because it is not necessary. My breasts are like tight little tennis balls, all perky and bouncy. I have no spare tires, front or back; just smooth supple skin. My long brown legs are cellulite free and my upper arms don't droop and jiggle when I reach up to pick a shiny, red apple. And my face, well, my face is absolutely radiant, chiseled chin and chicken neck now taut and trim. I look like Lauren Hutton without the gap.

There is nothing but open space for miles and miles and miles, rolling green grassy hills speckled with the odd tree. It is completely silent where I am. I do not see another soul. I do not hear anyone talking. In particular, I do not hear another foreign language—not Dutch—not French. Nothing. I am completely relaxed.

I affirm that I love myself unconditionally three times, take three teeny breaths through the cotton balls in my mouth, return to my Beta level of consciousness and take a refreshing look around.

Steve and Pete are now taking a breather after breakfast and we are having a three-way staring contest. It's me against their four black bee-bees. I blinked first, officially ending the contest which prompted them to celebrate their victory by having consensual sexual relations right in front of me.

During their furry cavorting around I swear I could sense a pesky hair pop out of my chin without any warning at all. Probably a menopausal hormone surge brought on by major fear and confusion. In this case it was my recent abduction and incarceration in what seemed to be an abandoned warehouse—cement floors, high ceilings, boarded up windows draped with sheer cobweb curtains. Except for the thin beam of light filtering through a crevice in the wall, which was serving as a spotlight for the performers in the live sex show now ending, the room was dark.

My attention to the rats was beginning to wane and thoughts of escape replaced my interest in their need to procreate. Noise coming from the adjoining room was building—sounded like voices and furniture being moved around. This new diversion took the rats over for a look-see as well as to seek out the possibility of more grub on the other side.

They were quickly bored I guess because they soon skittled back over to my side of the room. The next thing you know—with the crevice light serving as a spotlight once again—they unabashedly copulated *again* right in front of me. The actual "act" lasted about five seconds, start to finish. Then they ruffled their furry bodies at each other in what is probably rat talk for was-it-as-good-for-you-as-it-was-for-me and scurried away from where I was still reclining face down on the filthy floor.

Just when I thought the novelty of my presence had worn off, the satiated duo turned around again, darted behind me and leaped on my back. My first instinct was to shake them off but Something told me to be still. I felt their wooly bodies tickling my wrists and upper arms as they gnawed at my paisley vest, then finally, and you won't believe this, I sensed a slackening of my bonds.

Picture this: In the midst of slopping around on the scummy floor trying to get free, I apparently picked up a slab of discarded brie which had smeared across my back, and luckily, also on the ties that bound me. Petey and the newly renamed "Stephanie" chewed their way through the chintzy shoelaces holding my elbows together while enjoying the very mature brie crusted all over my arms and back— their second breakfast of the day, compared to my none. I guess rat-sex can make one ravenous.

My aching arms felt as if they didn't want to come back around front where they belonged. With a little effort I was eventually back in one straight line and able to unbutton the top three buttons of my 501's. I pulled out the dried up gag from my mouth then untied my legs. An unconscious quick check confirmed that yes, indeed, I had a new chin hair. The sleek patch on my ankle was still in place—one bright spot to the beginning of an otherwise lousy day. I checked the pockets of my *real* tight Misses size twelve black *Levi's* hoping that I had tucked away my trusty tweezers to pluck out the wiry hair but could only come up with two bobby pins, a mirror shard from my broken Cover Girl compact and two pulverized M&M's—one red, one yellow. I flicked the prickly little dickens back and forth as I looked around the room for an easy exit.

Pete and Stephanie left unceremoniously without waiting for an expression of my undying gratitude, but it was just as well, anyway. I didn't know how to go about thanking two fat brown rats for saving my life. Lifesaving rats. It could be a new show topic for Oprah: "French Rodents that Save Lives…Where Are They Now?"

Hey, Jokester up there…do You really have something to do with this? I prayed. I can't for the life of me understand why I am here. You do. Of course You do. Dearest Father, I would like to get home safely, if it is in Your plan, of course. If this is just a lesson teaching thing for me wanting to have a little fun, please forgive me and guide me out of this place at Your earliest convenience, preferably so I can take the 11 o'clock train back home today. Of course I'm Yours for whatever you would have me do for You. Wait a sec…I think I hear someth….never mind. Must be my wild imagination again. Lord, I know, I know I made a couple of bad decisions especially with that stupid Jacques guy. What's up with him anyway? Why in the world does he think I have some papers he is sooooo desperate for? What a jerk. Sorry. I know You love him too but You have to admit he has not been at all cordial since he doped me up last night. I just can't imagine why I'm here. I hate to ask for signs but if You have a hint you can share, I'd be most grateful…Amen.

I sat patiently in the dark, sucked on the linty M&M's and waited for a sign.

Before settling in Holland—and in between mothering—I had a not so brilliant career as a private investigator, thus my penchant for adventure. I never solved a case on my own. Maybe it was me. Maybe I was too cautious, too nervous or okay, maybe too inept to even come close. Well, I lie. I did come close once. A reporter for *"PSSS'T* Magazine," a third rate gossip rag, hired me to find out how his confidential sources were repeatedly being revealed to one of his arch rivals, a more upscale, second rate scandal sheet. Technically, I botched it up, but what I continue to hold on to was that I was this close to an investigative break through. The screw up was an accident. It could have happened to anyone. Big deal, so here's what happened: I fell off a twelve foot block wall while trying to adjust the audio control of my surveillance equipment. My fall was broken by about fifty pounds of duck pâté stuffed into a five foot round foccacio loaf—the would-be centerpiece of an elaborate luncheon table in ritzy-titzy Beverly Hills.

My fortuitous soft landing caused an unfortunate chain reaction, catapulting fifty melon fruit cups *way* up to the sky. The decked out garden party guests were consequently showered with juicy pastel balls descending from heaven. A heckuva colorful sight, but nevertheless my cover was blown, my assignment pulled and I got the proverbial hook.

There were other incidents convincing me to chuck it in, but life is too short to dwell on one's mistakes, so I moved on. Forced into premature retirement, I found a new life in Holland with Soul Mate.

First I thought middle-age mothering might be the way to go. At the age of forty one, Soul Mate and I created a beautiful combination of both of us—blond, blue-eyed Christina. Talk about a paradigm shift. As much as I cherish and adore my own sweet girl I am not what you'd call terribly maternal when it comes to other people's kids. That may be an overstatement, but let's just say—in general— delightful children's sounds that give most parents a warm, fuzzy feeling—such as uncontrollable bubbly laughter as a result of having too much fun—gets on my nerves.

Activity was increasing on the other side. Someone in pain. Maybe it was a torture chamber and I was the only one left in the waiting room. I unstuck the contact lens from my cheek, swirled it around my mouth to soften it up with what little spit I could muster, and carefully placed it in my right eye. The light filtering through the long, inch wide gap near the top up the decaying wall was my only hope to find out what the ruckus was all about. Instead of hustling my butt out of there, as a normal person would do, my old P.I. instinct was summoning me to the crack in the wall. But how could I reach? It was at least ten feet high. Utilizing whatever I could find in the room, I managed to secure two weakly constructed wine crates on top of each other to elevate my 5'7" frame to the bottom edge of the one inch gap. I tippy-toed up another two inches to get a better view.

Indeed, human misfortune in progress.

The glistening crowning of an infant caught my eye first. It was making its way out of a terrified teenage girl, who, at the moment I joined the scene, was in the middle of an intense contraction. She dug her matted head into the filthy mattress and *ughed* and *agghhhhed* her way right down to the hard floor where she vomited all over the place. Her two labor "coaches,"—also young with big bellies and panic stricken faces—carefully dragged the exhausted girl back to the center of the grubby cot, wiped the throw-up away from around her mouth and neck and comforted her back into place. Their own advanced stages of pregnancy made it difficult for them to hold down the writhing girl who was a few grunts away from increasing the population of France—like it or not. The three teens had a lot in common. None of it good. Being female and fertile was one thing. The other was the frozen expression of horror on their dirty little faces.

A short distance away, a doctor, or so it would seem by the obligatory white jacket, was observing the accelerating goings-on in this makeshift clinic in the middle of Nowhere, France. He looked Middle Eastern—brown skin, coarse dark hair that curled up at the nape of his neck, tall and, God, I hate to even say it—really good looking. He slouched over in a straddled position on a fold up metal Canasta chair. On the imitation Louis XIV lamp table in front of him was an ashtray chock-a-block full of one inch butts. A near empty bottle of Dewars sat on top of a stack of dog-eared papers.

Dr. Hunkanahalf was so plastered that he had a hard time keeping himself mounted on a chair that looked to me like just a regular chair. He swayed from one side to the other and every time he closed his eyes for a second he would throw his right leg out to catch himself, as if the chair was really a motorcycle in disguise and he was negotiating a hairpin curve at 100 mph. He was most definitely not in any condition to deliver one baby, let alone the other two, due any minute now. He took a final slug from the bottle, tapped the bottom to catch the last dribble, eyeballed down the neck to make sure there were no droplets stuck at the bottom and placed it reluctantly back on the pile of papers. Then he lit a new cigarette and tried to look official in his capacity as head of obstetrics.

A long, ululating moan and the fuzzy ball hiding between the trembling thighs of the child bearing a child pushed its way forward. I was fascinated to view childbirth from another vantage point and temporarily lost track of the situation at hand. I marveled about the wonder of new life, the wonderfulness of women in general and our ability to expel an object the size of a shucked coconut with the help of a few grunts. I unconsciously performed a couple of celebratory kegel exercises in our honor. Another mighty groan from the laboring child took me back six years ago to the moment my precious daughter left her own protective cocoon and entered the world.

Oh my God! Christina. My baby! I had to know what time it was, but how? My palms and fingertips were digging into the wall as if doing so would somehow relieve some of the taxing pressure of my size twelve-and-a-half-to-thirteen self to the weakening wine crates. I slowly released my left hand, causing the thin balsa slats to bend and creak under the uneven placement of my weight. I squinted hard to read the bitty hands on my watch. The crystal was shattered and the big hand was gone. The little hand was on the ten. It was ten whatever. Something crashed to the ground on the other side.

Probably the girl again. I carefully redistributed my size 12.75 self, dug into the wall and returned to the crack.

The motorcycle/chair appeared to have had a run in with the lamp table. The doctor was on his knees rearranging the scattered documents. He left the overturned ashtray and its contents on the ground, picked up the still in tact Dewars bottle and rested it sideways across the papers. With that done he remounted his Harley. The noise didn't seem to interfere with the girl on the dilapidated hospital bed. In between contractions she would conk out and the other two—the two with their own buns in the oven to worry about—leaned against the wall to rest as there were no other chairs in the room—save for the motorcycle one their drunk doctor was clinging to.

I was also knackered. It must have been more than twenty four hours since I woke up in my own cozy bed yesterday morning. So much has happened. Mostly bad. What in the hell was I thinking when I decided to take off?

The wandering thoughts of my daughter, my mundane life, my weight, the sex life of rodents and escape into relaxation therapy was interrupted by another frenzied wail coming from the pregnant girl.
I put my one good eye back into the spy hole.

Mama, cried the girl on the cot. *Maaaaa Maaaaaa,* she groaned through clenched teeth during a particularly rough contraction.

The drunken ob/gyn was now totally useless. The other two girls, tired and weeping, did their earnest best to help each other through the ordeal. One young thing was pale and delicate. Her dull beige hair was waist length, yet lackluster; split ends going right back to the roots. Everything about her was the same color. Beige. Her hair, skin, eyes, even her maternity sack was beige. The growth in front of her was so oversized for her body that she could hardly move around the bed to take the grasping hand begging for relief. She had been dealt a rough life, this little one. An anemic beige life that had seen better days than what is in store for her—from the looks of it—oh, probably by this time tomorrow.

She sobbed as she midwifed.

The other pregnant birthing attendant was a bit more hardy—just as petrified, but more able to take control of the situation, pleading with the laboring girl to stay calm and breathe. She was pretty, large boned, probably with Southern German blood, a squiggly patch of red hair, nearly colorless blue eyes, and a prominent belly resting so low that it looked as though she was also ready to go any minute.

Another pitiful cry and a long, pushing grunt.

I strained further to take in more of the atrocity unfolding on the other side but then my thoughts leaped to Christian...

Beautiful son, Christian—my go at teenage motherhood.

There's a twenty year gap between Christina and her *really* big brother, Christian. People think I'm kidding but I really mean it when I say God knew how to space my children. My boy turned out great. Six two, also blond with greenish blue eyes, a terrific smile, physique and sense of humor.

I worry less about Christian these days, but as a single mom raising a teenager in Southern California, we hit a rough patch around the age of fifteen. "OH MAAANN, I CAN NOT BUL-LIEVE YEW. YEW EMBARRASS ME SOOOO MUCH" and "YEW ARE SOOOOO WEIRD" were often used by Christian to express his frequent frustration with me. It was also during this phase that he began skipping school for days at a time if the surf was happening, dude. Then one awesome sunny day, the dean of the high school invited the potential future criminal and his parents to attend a three day Scared Straight seminar at the local Police Station, at which time we would be given statistics of what to expect from habitual truants: one minor arrest would lead to another, and another. Jail term. Rap sheet. Life of habitual crime. A gnarly prospect indeed. The dramatic conclusion to this effective shock therapy was a tour of the county jail—a tough place with even tougher tenants. This was a place no hunky blond surfer with a cute tush would want to spend even one long, but perhaps not so lonely night.

Christian made a fast turn around after that meeting. Today he owns a profitable commercial lobster fishing operation and recently married Angela, a delightfully earthy Italian girl. I will soon be entering my next life plateau—grandmother. I haven't brought it up yet but I am going to ask them if my little grandperson may be allowed to call me Darra. I think Darra has a much nicer ring to it and is easier for little mouths to wrap around...Da Da Darr-Darra. See? Way better than GRAAAND-AH-MOTHER.

Twenty years later, my second chance at mothering and Christina entered my life. I remember the first few moments after she arrived. It felt like we were engulfed in a heavenly cloud, full of warm and clean and safe. I must have had a maternal glow then because it was the first time I didn't worry if my hair looked frizzy or if the ample mass of pizza dough beneath my lactating breasts would ever totally go away. It didn't, by the way. We were in such a state of contented bliss that we used a line from an old Carpenter's song to express our joy in her birth announcements:

On the day that you were born
The angels got together
And decided to create a dream come true...

"Tell'er tu pooosh, goddamnit," the doctor barked incoherently.
His shrieking at the girls caused my often used mind escape capability to fail me and I was plopped back into reality. I felt sick. This young girl is not going to feel the right kind of warm, or clean, or safe when her innocent babe enters this sick-o world to meet its mom. No. This mom won't have a maternal glow, nor does she even know what it is. She's a kid.

For an instant, I wished she were mine. If she were mine I could use my supermothersonic power to rip through the wall that separates us, grab my baby having a baby and get the hell out of there, only taking enough time to turn around to kill the motherf—-ing doctor, then Jacques and Hank on my way out. I would take over as labor coach for the last crucial minutes, look deep into her eyes with unconditional mother love, convincing her that everything would be all right. And it would be. Her babe would know from its first breath that it was loved and wanted.

I would do that if I was her mother. It's a kind of special power gift we have. Like lifting a one ton car off your child's legs while not being able to unscrew the lid on a peanut butter jar without help. It's like in "Terms of Endearment" when Shirley MacLaine flips out in the hospital when the nursing staff is yakking away and misses the exact scheduled time for her dying daughter's dose of pain killer. A minute—even a nanosecond of unnecessary pain to a mother's child is unbearable. Only a mother's heart could ache every time she watches that scene.

At this very moment I realize I am maternal. Hey.

Trouble is I'm not *her* mother. That's the difference. Unfortunately, in my case these extraordinary mother powers are not transferable. I can not do it. I can not save her.

I'm frozen in fear as well as shame.

My strained right eye connects with the very farthest corner of the room. My former unsuspecting captors, the French Odd Couple, just entered and were anxiously looking on. Jacques was still fresh as a daisy, no unplanned wrinkles or unsightly perspiration lines in his silk shirt, and Hank, well, I caught Hank fingering a blackhead on his cheek that must have been housed on his face so long that with the right amount of pressure it could jump right out, thus initiating his long overdue beauty overhaul. Wishful thinking. With no doubt the crater left by its former occupant would fill up again, and again, until the next time. I'm sure he hadn't bathed since he left this room not long ago so I am also sure he stills reeks of B.O.

They were fidgeting around, hands in and out of pockets, talking with enthusiastic animation back and forth to each other like expectant fathers waiting to compare birth weights and pass out cigars. Except I knew better. I put my ear to the hole in the wall but they were inconveniently speaking in that foreign tongue again.

Directly opposite Felix & Oscar and closer to me but in an awkward line of vision was yet another shocking sight—a cubbyhole corner nursery consisting of two newborns. They lay wrapped in brand new pastel pink, blue and yellow striped receiving blankets in small blue bassinets that looked like they doubled as carriers. Amid the squalor of the room, this little corner could almost pass for clean. There was a three foot high room partition separating the infants from the activity going on just a few feet away. They didn't cry. Not for no-reason-at-all like all babies do. Just not at all. In the midst of all the confusion going on in the room, they slept soundly. Weird.

Also fast asleep on the floor near the nursery was a heavy set woman around sixty years old. She was curled up in an apropos fetal position on top of a Snow White & The Seven Dwarfs sleeping bag. I could only see that she was also Middle Eastern, thick black hair with the occasional steel wire running through it. Drool ran down the corner of her moustached framed mouth, made a left turn when it hit a mound of hairy flesh and continued to meander its way down the flabby neck before settling on the damp, quilted face of Dopey. I hadn't decided yet if she was with the bad guys or not. A blond, curly head that I made out to be around a year and half old was nestled into her ample breasts. Also asleep.

I didn't see any new mothers. Only three empty bassinets waiting to be filled.

I didn't know how much more I could take without busting down the place but then an unfamiliar feeling of confidence and determination took over and the Plan To Save These Poor Souls, as well as my own fanny, went into action.

The Plan did not include busting down the place.

As I stepped down from the pile of faithful wine crates and slipped out of the carelessly unlocked door, I heard the pathetic whimper of two babies—that of the frightened mom and the other of the fragile new life she just gave. I couldn't hang around to see if it was a boy or girl. I guess it didn't even matter.

Outside of the prison-slash-baby hospital was the middle of nowhere. Nobody around. No noise. Sort of like the quiet places I visit when I travel to the Alpha level of my of my mind during my relaxation exercises. But this place was not peaceful or beautiful. It was sinister and spooky and even though I knew I'd have to come back, right now I wanted outta' there.

I just started running. Like a bat outta' hell I ran. I was pretty sure I was still in Paris, or the vicinity of, but nothing looked familiar. There were rows and rows of rusty oil barrels, miles of six inch round steel cables, some abandoned old cars and four or five rickety old buildings, probably used for similar unscrupulous purposes at one time or another.

I ran for about five minutes noting landmarks on my way—a retired auto salvage yard next to a deserted one pump gas station with a sign boasting *ouvert tous les jours* hung from the door of an unmanned pay booth—a heap of compost or some sort of decaying matter dumped on the side of the road. If nothing else, I thought, I might be able to sniff my way back here. Then I reached an unpaved road, not very busy at this time of day, or probably any time of day. Well, I didn't even know what time of day it was but the sun was not yet overhead. Sometime today Jacques had to deliver the "shipment" and "papers" to some guy called Mabouk.

Duh. V-8 time again.
Shipment: Babies.
Papers: Birth certificates.

But how did I—meaning my double, fit in?

The fifth car stopped to pick me up. And what a relief. The four preceding cars not only did not contemplate stopping, but, in fact, had whizzed by me with such hasty and cowardice flight that the dry dirt road seemed to turn into an endless dust bowl highway. Brown clouds powdered me from head to toe.

Monsieur LaPointe must have been feeling mighty adventurous today. I'm an easy frump under ideal situations, so I guess I must have looked a fright. I had sneaked an underarm whiff while waiting for a ride, so when this miniature cartoon car—a Fiat 500—pulled over, I tried an inconspicuous arm flap to air out before I actually got in to meet the good Samaritan who took a chance on me.

Monsieur LaPointe was a hygienic version of Hank. He looked like a farmer or a rural sort of Frenchman, red plaid shirt with a frayed collar, charcoal gray Polyester Pete slacks with a permanent crease, a light blue hand-knitted vest and dirty Nikes. He, or his shoes, had a faint aroma of cow dung, therefore my farmer-going-to-town deduction.

His diminutive stature endeared him to me somehow. His hands looked like a great ad idea for Hormel Vienna sausages—A little animated character in Monsieur LaPointe's likeness dancing around like a munchkin singing *They're finger lickin' good!* as he bit off each Vienna finger sausage one at a time with a silly grin on his face. Then of course these finger sausages would instantly pop right back because it's a cartoon after all. It's like when Roadrunner is forever flattening Wile E. Coyote with huge boulders or steam rollers. Five seconds later Wile E. is puffed up to normal and back in action. Same principle.

Monsieur LaPointe had approximately 237 strands of dark brown hair methodically placed on his head—each one smidged with a little dab o' Brylcreem to insure its security in its designated spot. Every strand is totally aware of where it is required to remain until moved by its master, unless, God forbid, a violent *mistral* blew in to town without warning. Then all hell hair chaos would break loose and we'd be dealing with one frantic little Frenchman.

I thought he was kinda' cute but that's probably because he had become part of my growing rescue team: Stephanie, Pete, and now, the Farmer LaPointe.

He spoke to me in French. I spoke to him in English. We didn't understand what in the hell the other was saying. To break the silence at one point, I repeated the only long sentence in French I could recall which was something like:

Voolay vu kou-shay avek mwah say swahr?

He smiled so I guess my pronunciation was on target. I went on:

Paris. Place St-Michel.

He said, *oui, oui, Place St-Michel,*

Hotel. I said.

Oui, 'otel, he said. His eyes rolled.

46

And then with some help from my hands I said, *Sleep.*

Oui, oui, zleep, he said. Eye roll.

Money. I pay you.

Oui, oui, mahney, he said. No eye roll.

Take me there, Puullleeeze.

Oui, oui, oui, 'otel, sleeeep, mahney, he repeated exuberantly.
'Otel, sleeeep, mahney.

Sometimes my pleading tactic does work. He got a glint in his rolling eyes and floored the gas.

After a twenty minute drive that consisted of three times tried and three times failed attempts by Monsieur LaPointe to massage my left inner thigh, I realized that sign language can sometimes give off double meanings. Another language hurdle I did not have the time or energy to deal with.

Fortunately, there is never a convenient place to park around Place St-Michel, or anywhere close to my hotel. So, once again, with my hands, I told Monsieur LaPointe that while he was finding a parking spot, I would walk ahead to my hotel, the Hotel du Vieux on rue Gît-le-Coeur, room #6, freshen up, and wait for him to come up for his reward. Heh. Heh.

And then I walked to my real hotel.

It looked like Marcel's replacement hadn't shown up since he was where I left him a lifetime ago. Same book. Probably same page—rereading one particularly graphic depiction of the endless possibilities of overcoming boredom while living on a farm. Farmer LaPointe could give him a few personal pointers of his own, I'm sure.

I reached over the side of the desk, took my breadboard key holder from its designated hook, tiptoed to the stairs, vaulted two at a time to the third floor, then ran to the nearest toilet to pee like a race horse.

My room was as I left it. Depressing. The faded chartreuse velvet look wallpaper was coming apart on all four corners of the ceiling. The faux marble topped bedside table had a drawer that had been crookedly jammed shut and a useless narrow cupboard that reminded me of my cozy clothes closet back home. It stood on three stubby two inch legs. The fourth leg had been sloppily amputated and replaced blasphemously with a holy prosthesis, the guest room bible.

My bed, surely the site of numerous baby-making rehearsals, was covered with a well-worn dark red chenille spread with a coordinating trim of chartreuse balls with red speckles. I noted that almost all cheap hotel rooms have dark spreads to hide stains.

Ewwwww. I jumped off the bed.

My mind was going every which way. I had a major problem on my hands yet somehow I used up two valuable minutes to do a quality room inspection for the hotel housekeeping department. I had to get my wits about me. I pushed my bed up against the door for safety, pulled down the bedspread and collapsed on the suspect sheets to get ready for a three minute trip to my mind's Alpha level of consciousness. I needed to do something to gather strength to go on.
Before I closed my eyes I caught sight of three curly Timex watch springs on the bottom sheet just waiting to disgust me. Either these bedclothes had not been changed since the last guest, or Marcel had been combing his hair over my bed. *Ewwwww.*

Whatever. It didn't matter anymore. I closed my eyes, took three deep breaths, imagined my entire body was a bowl of *al dente* tagliatelle as I reached my Alpha level and my quiet place.

My quiet places change. This time I was on a gigantic floating cotton puff of a cloud, nothing but warm blue skies that go on and on and on and on…I am lounging on a chartreuse satin chaise longue, crispy white eyelet pillows cushioning my lithe body. I am dressed in a slinky egg white Givenchy gown—backless of course, except for the four skinny straps playfully crisscrossing each other to meet at my slim waist. My hair is also white, styled in a swishy blunt cut, not in the slightest bit frizzy, and my face, although still beautiful, has a mature, serene aura about it.

I am a grandmother. A beautiful grandmother.

A group of rambunctious four year olds with raspberry jam sandwiches and full glasses of grape Kool-Aid chase each other around my chaise longue. I think it's cute. Their laughter is music to my ears. They are having too much fun! I welcome their grape jelly fingered hugs and strawberry jam kisses as I browse through the latest issue of "Grandparent World". I become even more relaxed as I sew twelve Mother-of-Pearl buttons on the back of Bridal Barbie's formal wedding gown.

I take a deeper breath and see a fifteen year old blond boy carrying a surfboard, coming closer and closer. We smile lovingly at each other. He sits at the end of my chaise and we have a nice chat. I listen to him. He listens to me. He shares the events of the day along with his innermost feelings about just about everything, while I listen. Then he listens intently as I tell him how much I love him and how much having him in my life, while perhaps not always so apparent, means to me.

He believes me.

Nothing could be more rewarding. I have reached the epitome of contentment—a combination of beauty, patience, love and understanding.

I am totally relaxed. I affirm that I love myself unconditionally, take three deep breaths, stretch my arms over my head, open my eyes and come out of the Alpha and back into the Beta.

Back to reality. Although this last exercise has helped somewhat, it is not enough to avoid the mini-breakdown I knew was inevitable. I felt it coming.

It always starts the same way. A slow rumbling somewhere down in the stomach that turns into a moaning animal sound deep inside trying to get out. It quickly escalates to a silent scream where the mouth opens wide and you look a lot like the subject in Edvard Munck's famous painting, "The Scream". You feel pain, feel despair, but nothing comes out. Or—you babble bab-bab-bab sounds and blow bubbles with the excess saliva without even trying. Your eyes glass over and stare straight ahead at nothing. You want to muffle yourself but you can't. You have no say anymore. You are temporarily out of control. You are crazy. I am crazy. I have a deranged expression across my face, which always scares me if I look in a mirror. If I do make the mistake of looking in a mirror, I am so frightened that I fall into a conditional catatonic state. By conditional I mean I fall into it but probably could snap out of it if, let's say, the room was on fire. I worry about one day not coming out of it. To be certified mad. To go to a nut house and be left to die in Holland before I ever get to move home, to move back to America, like Soul Mate promised we would someday. I really worry about that.

I want to go home.

I haven't had a mental collapse like this in a long time, but the events of the past twelve hours had broken me. I still ached all over but more in my heart than anywhere else. I grabbed the Bible holding up the bedside table, clutched it to my chest and pledged to God that if he would give me the power to save these children, as well as myself, I would surely make it up to my children, as well as their children, and well, all right, even those bratty kids in my neighborhood back home.

I think He went along with the deal.

For the first time since returning to my room twenty minutes ago, I checked the mirror to see why all those cars refused to stop for me on the highway. What was the big tah-doo all about anyway?

Well, shoot. My face and hair were a right mess. Eyebrows gone, mole gone, lipstick long gone. The only make-up that managed to at least stay on my face was my non-smudge mascara, which made its way down both cheeks to give me an Alice Cooper in a frosted wig look.

You can't do much to damage black jeans, but when I looked down to see that they were still in their comfort relief mode I apologized in my heart to Monsieur La Pointe for giving him mixed signals. My wrinkled white blouse was now a wrinkled mocha blouse. Strangely, the paisley vest seemed to be still in tact so I took it off and was about to hang it on the back of the ladder back chair when I got a whiff of the same strong scent of cow manure I noticed when I got into Monsieur La Pointe's Fiat. When I flipped the vest over I saw that it, as well as my Levi's, was coated with yellow, *very* mature brie.

It appeared that I had accused Monsieur LaPointe unjustly on a couple of counts. And worse, he was still wandering around the entire 14th Arrondissement looking for me and his reward.

I took a short, hot shower taking along my smelly clothes to wash away some of the odor. I did a half-assed blow job on my wet hair which means it came out in an undesirable frizz. Sort of an Afro really. An Afro is an unflattering style on just about everyone, but even more so on mature women. Back in the 70's, every woman over thirty had an Afro. They assumed that because it was a politically correct hairdo and young people wore them, they too, would become young, hip, groovy. They'd be able to relate better to their Afro'ed teenagers because they were on the same level. Hairdo wise, that is. You'd see these little ol' housewives in their burgundy polyester flares and matching burgundy and navy blue flowered tops from the Sears catalog, white platform sandals and—an Afro. In my day, a status symbol item would be an Fro comb dangling from your key chain. Today I sported an unplanned Afro. Not a groovy look on me. Not in the 70's. Not now. Not ever.

I had only packed one other outfit so the choice was easy—black leggings and a giant black designer T-shirt that I picked up in Hong Kong on a layover three years ago. It had a gold CHANEL with two huge crossed "C's" emblazoned across the front—the "C's" authenticating the shirt as being a *genuine* CHANEL. I got a really good price for it and proudly left the Hong Kong market knowing that I made the deal of the decade.

I slipped on my black leather flats over black knee-hi's, then to bring it all together, I dabbed from the sample flacon of Chanel No. 5 leaking from my toilet bag. Thank God I found an extra pair of contacts in the bag as well as my trusty Twizzors, giving me the much needed opportunity to catch up on my new crop of chin sprouts. I stepped back to access my new look but let's face it, it was not a new look. Leggings and oversized shirts have been out for years. I've been in a fashion time-warp and never knew it—or could admit it—until this very minute. I looked in the mirror and saw the chunksy mother of Batman wearing a frizzy yellow crash helmet.

I have just GOT to get a handle on my personal appearance when I get back home, I relayed to my reflection. First, I'm gonna dump all the clothes in my cozy closet and start all over again with a few basics—a few mix and match classic separates that I can wear for at least ten years. Something flattering and slimming. Something Chanel-ish maybe. Something that says timeless elegance. I can't wait. I'll be gorgeous.

And another thing—forget this bogus Sleek Patch idea. I'm going to sign up at Bernadette's gym on Monday morning. Okay, okay, my feeble excuse for not joining a gym before now is that unlike the majority of men, I hate the "bouquet" of perspiring women. The last aerobics class I went to had about fifty-five women and three men burning their buns, but the room was in blatant violation of California Fire Code Number 72448, exceeding the room maximum occupancy by at least thirty over heated exercise freaks. That's a lot of sweat.
But then, these classes are the same all around the world:

Facing the class is the instructor, sometimes genuinely young, sometimes my age hiding out in a teenage body—the giveaway being the detailed Los Angeles Freeway system map routed to Old Ladydom across her face. She's calling out,

Annnd ah 4-3-2-1 annnnnd again 3-2-1…. one more time, 2-1….
They always depress me, these instructors.

Then there's the hard babes in the front row. Like they really need to be there. The next row is reserved for the gals who do indeed need to be there but don't think they do. They wear those killer thong things that disappear into the folds of their butt and they act like it doesn't bother them. I guess they are there to provide comic relief. The rows behind are filled with descending levels of body shapeliness, ending with the back row, which on my one and only visit, I shared with a grossly overweight and consequently highly glandular woman who was taking advantage of a one free visit coupon cut out of her local newspaper. On the other side of me was an octogenarian with a sky blue hairdo that didn't budge when she jumped or when she jacked. She could have been a lead hard babe in the front row if she had only started fifty years earlier. She also made me depressed. I couldn't keep up with her. Then—there are the men who always seem to find themselves directly behind a hard babe in a thong. I don't know. In my opinion, all those moist bottoms undulating up and down two inches away from their exercising neighbors is nothing less than hard floor sex moving to the pulsation of *"She Works Hard For Her Money"*.

Uh. Uh. No thank you. Once is enough. I can do it alone. I'm going to get into lifting weights, body sculpting. Yep. I'll compete in the Ms. Buns Of Steel 2002 contest that I saw advertised in Muscle Madness last month.

In ardent defiance, I peeled off the Sleek Patch barely hanging on my right ankle, slapped it on the flattering bathroom mirror and marched out the door.

Feeling Strong. Feeling Woman. Feeling Invincible…

Eight

My first stop was the dreaded reception area where I was pleasantly surprised to find Claude. I was sure Claude would remember me from my last visit when we had a two minute quality conversation on where I could find the best exchange window to convert my Dutch guilders to francs. Claude is a cherubic little mole of a man with a rosy cheeked beach ball head, wavy gray hair, tiny ears, thin lips, button nose and sweet little doe brown eyes. His neck, or lack of it, disappeared into a black turtleneck. He was also reading but his literature of choice was a bit more conservative than Marcel's. He was skimming through Paris Match, the French version of People Magazine. I sure was glad to see him. I gave him my brightest smile, adding a wiggle of my newly filled in brows and mole and in typical, friendly Americanese said:

Hiaaaahhhhyeeee, Claude. It's me. Remember me? Darra. I live in Holland but I'm American and I come here a coupla' of times a year just to get away from, you know, HOLLAND, and hey, how's it goin? You look grrreat, Claude. I mean it. Did you do something to your hair? I mean you really look great. Really different. Different in a good way, I mean.

Claude looked up when I was about half way through my sincere greeting, gave me an vacant stare and when I was through rambling, said,

Oui? Qui' est ce que vous voulez?

What do I want? You want to know what do I w a n t? I'll tell you what I want, you little roly-poly wart hog. What I want is for one day to come to Paris and leave feeling like I had a face. A face someone, anyone, would remember. That's what I want.

I didn't actually go into sharing that frustration with him. I just said, *Si vu play...telephon-o Amer-i-co* and politely gave him my MCI phone card to patch me through to Christian's number in California. When my son's voice came on the line I chattered about how I missed him so much and wanted to see him soon and that I loved him and that, gee, I hope we could get to see each other for Christmas this year and did he get my letter...but before I could remind him to wear his seat belt and make sure he had a designated driver when he went out with his friends, the answering machine's beep interrupted my message so I hung up. I couldn't remember the last time I actually heard Christian's voice first hand. I gave Claude my number in Bozum to talk to Christina and to check in with Marielle. I hummed "Cat's in the Cradle" under my breath while I waited and thumbed through a "Paris la Nuit" Where to Go Guide.

I needed to hear my little girl's voice, to make sure she was okay. I couldn't get Christian or Christina off my mind since witnessing that appalling childbirth scene at the warehouse this morning.

Christina answered the phone.

Hi mama. You know what? The most a-maz-ing thing happened yesterday at school. You want to know what? It was just a-maz-ing.

"Amazing" is Christina's new word-of-the-week.

I took my new Glitter Beach Barbie to school cause remember it was Toy Day at school and Martine and Linda both had Glitter Beach Barbie's just like mine 'cept Martine's had a blue bathing suit but I don't like blue and Linda's had a gorgeous purple bathing suit and my Barbie's bathing suit is orange but I wish I had Linda's cause I like purple better. It's my favorite lovely color. Can you buy me another Glitter Beach Barbie but this time with a purple bathing suit? When are you coming home, Mama? Marielle won't let me sleep with the light on in my room will you tell her to let me sleep with the light on? Mama? Oh, Mama, just great. Guess what. Poppa called and he said he had a surprise for us. Isn't that great? When are you comin' home?

Oh, sweetie pie, I'll be home pretty soon, I promise and I have a surprise for you too, I ad-libbed. *We'll see about a new Barbie, okay?* The kid has enough Barbies to populate a small town. *I better talk to Marielle to make sure she leaves the light on in your room. Of course you can have the light on. Let me talk to her, okay? I love yeeewwwww. Daaag.*

When Marielle came on the line, I kept up with my dying aunt story, and felt her out about the possibility of being a tad bit later than I arranged. Of course it was all right she said. I reminded her to leave Christina's light on in her bedroom when she tucked her in and asked her to tape the weekend double episode of "As The World Turns" with the blank cassette in the VCR cabinet. Just as she rang off, she passed on the message that by the way, Soul Mate phoned from Dallas and indeed he had a surprise for us. Oh, goody.

I talked to Christina one more time because she had a very important question to ask me. She wanted to know if God has a belly button.

My next stop was Café Aux Deux Magots, where this mysterious other woman bumped me once and changed my life forevermore.

Bun jur, I said with my limited language skills to the friendliest looking waiter in the café. I didn't know how to explain in French that the woman I was searching for looked like me, or to ask if he had seen anyone looking like me but perhaps more fashionably dressed.

So I showed him a wallet size family photo taken when I was wearing a reasonably stylish mango mohair suit, Christina on my lap, Soul Mate and Christian standing in the rear. *This woman,* I pointed. *Do. You. Know. This. Wo-man?*

Non.

Silly me. How did I expect them to remember a face like hers when no one in this city seems to remember mine?

Mer-cey for nothing, I thought but of course didn't say.

I sat down to get a grip on what to do next and immediately remembered that I had not eaten since last night when I had that cheese omelette. Funny, I thought, last night at Le Pêtite Chat I invited myself into other people's lives because I was bored and it was a safe, not to mention cheap, form of entertainment. But now, less than twenty four hours later, I was involved in a crime I couldn't walk away from even if I wanted to. The sight of those three pathetic little pregnant girls and the infants sleeping in the corner of the room would be with me as long as I live.

While waiting to order, I leaned against the partition separating the glassed in terrace and absorbed some of the sunshine we don't get in Holland. Surprisingly, my friendly garçon promptly noticed me as a paying customer, and strolled off relatively quickly with my request for the *plat du jour,* the Choucroute Garni, and a large *jus du orange*. I could have used a belt of vodka in my O.J. but I knew I had a lot of work ahead of me today and needed a clear head.

No, hon. You multiply 108 francs by 5, not divide. If you divide, that means one cafe au lait, one beer and two Croque Monsieurs cost $21.60 and that can't be right. If we mul-ti-ply then they are, let's see, let's see, don't talk to me while I'm calculating...just a sec. That meansssss, if we mul-ti-ply, like I think is right, then your cup of coffee, my beer, and two stupid grilled cheese sandwiches cost...$540.00. No, wait, that can't be right. Don't talk to me. If we di-vide....You're makin' me nervous, hon. Let me do it again. I think I *got it. JUST A MINUTE. Oh frig, I don't know. Just forget it. Just give the guy a traveler's check and see how much we get back.*

Bob and Betty Beasley, also known as Hon and Hon, were sitting at the little round table touching mine so I couldn't help eavesdropping even if I was not so inclined. But I am, so I did.

American tourists are always the easiest to single out without hearing them speak. It's the clothes. It's the grooming. It's the hair. It's the teeth. It's the make-up. It's the jewelry. It's the manicures. And, most of all, it's the sensible walking shoes, which I know all travel guides advise, but what they don't mention is that Europeans only wear sports shoes in the gym or when sporting. When in doubt, look at their shoes. That's what I do.

Anyway, Betty, around my age, was all of the above and then some. She was wearing a turquoise and salmon crushable velour running suit with a matching salmon T-shirt underneath the zip up jacket in case she got hot but wanted to stay matched up. She had a Bashful Blonde Roux rinse on her perfectly coiffed hairdo—a cotton candy hardhat helmet with two side wings. She must have heard about the many French films shooting practically every day in and around Paris, because the pancake and blush was nothing short of camera ready, and she was ready, honey.

Her long nails were done just before leaving for the airport yesterday. I wondered where in Paris she would find an Emergency Acrylic Nail Repair Center if it became necessary in the next ten days. Not my problem, I told myself. She was dripping in silver and turquoise. Two inch silver arrow points with turquoise beads threaded through the rod of the arrow for earrings, about six turquoise and silver bangle bracelets and a giant American Eagle pendant with strands of turquoise and coral beads, thus making the tie in with the salmon in her outfit—jingle jangling from his spread eagle wings.

Oh, and brand new, sensible white Adidas—a turquoise decorative strip crossing the logo.

American men, on the other hand, are sometimes more difficult to spot. You usually have to hear them speak or even gesture, like the simultaneous handshake and squeeze of the opposite shoulder greeting. *Hey, howyadoin, Buddy? Yadoinallright? Grrreat. That's grreat.*

Bob—tan of skin, white of teeth, bald of head, with a slight paunch advertising his age and alcohol persuasion, looked relatively fit. He was dressed in precision creased khaki pants, a pastel pink starched collar shirt with a white tennis sweater sporting the logo of some Native American Indian sounding Golf & Country Club. Something like Hohokum or Okhohee. Couldn't read it. Through probably no choice of his own, he was also into Indian jewelry—a silver chain with a broken arrow charm dangled from his copper neck, twisted silver arm bands with oval turquoise stones in the center circled both wrists, and on his ring finger—you got it—a golf ball size turquoise stone ring. Oh, and brand new white Nikes.

I took a wild stab and placed Bob and Betty as residents of the Southwest; Arizona or New Mexico would be a safe guess.

I snoop further:

So, where to now, hon? Betty.

I don't care, hon. I'll leave it up to you. You're the boss. I'm just along for the ride. Bob.

Well, it's one thirty now. We have to be back at the hotel by two thirty to meet Sue and Dick if we are going to try to get to the Louvre before it closes at 4:30. What do you think, hon? Do you think we ought to try to catch that Seine River cruise that Ned and Peg told us not to miss? It looks like here on the map to be about a quarter of an inch away, however far that is. Are you up to walking, hon? We've already walked a lot this morning. Howya feelin'? Let's do. Let's go on the boat and relax. We don't have to look at the sights if we don't want to. I mean let's be honest, hon, all these old buildings look alike, don't they? And they're so dirty besides. Anyhow, just as long as we don't leave here tomorrow without seeing that Mona at the Louvre. That would be really missing Paris, I think. Whattaya think, Bobby? Wanna go on a boat ride?

*I'm with ya, babe. Just let me hitch up my fanny pack, put the camcorder and all this other paraphernalia away and I'm all set. Let's see, did we pay yet? Did you leave a tip? What's the deal on that? Do we have to? Hell, let's just bolt. This clown doesn't like his job anyway. He's nothing like Brock or Derek at The Brassiere back home, is he? I mean, back home, now that's a real French restaurant, know what I mean? This guy, someone bettah tell im' he's never gonna make it as a waiter with an attitude like that. I tell ya, he's nevah gonna make it, that guy. Someone otta give him a "tip" all right. That's to remind him of the definition of T.I.P.S. **T**o **I**nsure **P**rompt **S**ervice. Someone's gotta teach him a lesson. Ya ready, hon? Let's go. But, hey, put that damn map away first. You want everyone to think we're tourists?*

The four white sensible shoes toddled off in the wrong direction just as I had polished off the last hunk of sausage and sauerkraut and wiped my plate clean with a piece of bread. Just like the French do.

Nine

Wacko minds like mine can split up into lots of divisions and sub-divisions when necessary. While I was eating and joining in on the Beasley's whirlwind Paris itinerary and their harsh restaurant service critique, I was making mental notes about what facts I had on the woman.

First of all, it was just about this time yesterday when she rushed out of here. I tried to detail everything I could remember about her apart from the fact that her face was like mine. She was my age but there was a distinct difference. Her hair? No. It was also blond and stylish—as mine was just yesterday. Her height and weight? Oh, about the same. Okay, a little less weight. Besides, expensive clothes always flatter a figure...

That's it! Her clothes! She was wearing an expensive suit, unlike my thrown together separates. It was a Chanel, or a Chanel wannabe. It was pink. That's all I remember. Pink and black maybe, sort of like the one Jackie Kennedy wore in Dallas on November 22, 1963.

The fleeting glimpse I had of the woman gave me the impression that she was not a knock-off designer shopper, so I paid up my lunch tab and followed my first real hunch. I started down boulevard St-Germain, turning right when I reached rue du Bac and straight across the Pont Royal, the end of Jardin des Tuileries, across rue du Rivoli, and finally rue du Faubourg St-Honoré, the chic area to shop the famous fashion houses of Paris—Guy LaRoche, Hermès, LaCroix, and Givenchy. I did not see the House of Chanel.

Timewise, I should have taken the Métro, because even at this fast clip it still took a good twenty minutes to reach the corner of rue du Faubourg St-Honoré and the rue de L'Elysee. I rested for a minute and deliberated the extent of how lost I was. Sometimes I think I know my way around this city but at least once during a visit I get discombobulated and have to resort to asking some French person for directions. The problem is, if I can get them to understand my query in French, they answer me back in French so I just say *Mer-see* and walk away just as confused—and lost.

As it turns out, this is one of those discombobulating times. I don't know if I should be turning left or right on this rue so I stop the first person I see, a dignified pensioner with a Salvador Dali moustache overlapping the sides of his face.

Bun-jur, Missyour, ew say trouve Chanel? Jahy zwee per-due.

I think I asked him...*where is Chanel? I am lost.*

Ah, oui, la maison Chanel. Attendez une minute. He twirled one rigid curly-Q with his left hand and with the other he tapped the cover of his silver watch farb as if it were a compass he might have to call on for assistance. He continued....*Nous sommes rue du Faubourg St.-Honoré. La maison Chanel, est la—tout doit, puis à gauche dans la rue Cambon, et, voilà!, c'est là. Facile. Comprenez-vous?*

See what I mean?

I said *mer-see missyour* as he sauntered away in the opposite direction, twirling away and pleased to have aided a lost visitor in his fair city.

Fortunately, he also used a little of that hand language business that got me in trouble with Monsieur LaPointe, so I made off in the general vicinity he had pointed to, hoping that soon I would be turning left at a small street coming up. *Oui, tres facile.*

Speaking of Monsieur LaPointe, as I crossed the rue Royale for the second time, I thought I saw him cruising past me one street up, on the rue Duphot, which turned out to be the street just in front of the one I was looking for. Poor guy, I mused. He really did save my ass and what did I do to thank him? Diddley squat. Now look at him. He's still driving around Paris trying to find a parking place. I slowed down my pace so he'd be gone by the time I reached the intersection.

Small world.

A few more minutes of disorientation and I found myself in front of the House of Chanel, a clean white building, simple elegance screaming from the crystal crossed C's door handles. I discreetly touched up my make up, blusher, lipstick and mole, then threw my shoulders back, forced my udders up, tucked my tummy in like my mom taught me, and flung open the double doors with a thud. Damn. I found out too late that the flashy doors with their signature handles didn't require much force, so my entrance, while not graceful, was certainly evident. This was like ten times the magnitude of making a walking mistake by a trendy café. Two saleswomen turned to the door, raised their eyebrows, glared, tsked, and went back to their classy customer already wearing a la-dee-dah Chanel outfit.

Inside the House of Chanel was black and white and gold with runway fashion show videos blaring from at least four televisions around the large room. Every two inches hung yet another logo buttoned and chain belted suit or coat or shoe or Lord only knows what else. I didn't check the underwear department—if there was one, but no doubt their trademark undies would be draped in tiny strands of golden chains, and logo buttons probably replaced the traditional hook and eye of their French cut under wire brassieres.

While I waited for one of the two salesgirls to come over to me, I poked around the racks looking for something to start my new wardrobe. I could not believe the prices. Maybe I was calculating francs to guilders to U.S. dollars in my head wrong. A lacquered black table close to the entrance displayed short, neat piles of T-shirts, some white with black logos, and some like mine, black with big gold "C's". I thumbed through them as if I were a legitimate customer and not a comparison shopper. I could hardly contain my smug expression when I saw that they were asking $200 for *almost* the exact same T-shirt I got in Hong-Kong for $19.95! The only difference was the direction in which the "C's crossed. Big deal.

Like I said, there were two—not one, but two salespersons assisting this attractive customer in her early thirties, obviously with big francs to spend. Yet nobody had approached me and I had been there for well over ten minutes. That's what gets me. How in the world do they expect you to dress nice and look nice if nobody helps you? Nobody pays attention to you. I mean, if I had walked in with one of their creations already on my back, they'd be all over me like flies by now. Guaranteed. But no, I'm only wearing one of their $200—*heh heh*—T-shirts and that doesn't qualify me for prompt service. And I am very serious about dumping my clothes at home and starting over with a few Chanel things. But they don't have to know that. They need to treat me just like they are treating Madame Rich Bitch over there. Just wait until they do decide to assist me. I'll tell them what I think.

Bonjour, Madame, puis-je vous aider?

I turned around. We looked at each other as if in a mirror. It was obvious she didn't notice the resemblance when she collided into my table yesterday, because she was now shocked for the first time. For me, I was surprised at having a hunch pay off the first time around even though I was searching for her as a customer of Chanel, not a salesperson.

She did look exactly like me, only aging better. And why not? She wore expensive make-up and perfume. She looked like she wouldn't know what to do in a kitchen except maybe how to slice a cucumber for a refreshing eye mask. In fact, I suspected she'd had a tuck here and there. Not to mention her endless designer wardrobe. Today it was a black number with all kinds of distinguishing gold logo buttons and chain belts from top to bottom. I found it a little much.

Meow. Meow. I know, I know it sounds terribly catty, but I don't mean that way. Looking at her actually encourages me and gives me hope for what I could be if I tried. Really.

Hi, I said. *Do you speak English?*

I was tired of struggling with French and watching the glazed look come over my conversation partner's eyes. I've been getting that look from Dutch people for seven years and I came to Paris to take a vacation from it.

Mais oui. I mean, yes of courze. May I be of azziztanze?, she asked without knowing just how much she would be assisting me in the next few minutes.

Yes, I replied. *But, I'm not here to shop. Well, I mean, I am. Eventually. But at the moment, I have a pressing problem that I hope you will be able to help me with.*

Me? she said with a quizzical look. *How iz it pozzible zhat I can I help you?*

Well, for starters...

"For starterz?" What meanz "for starterz?"

Oh, sorry. I'll try to leave out the slang.

"Zlang"? What meanz ze "zlang"?, she said with an even more puzzled expression that distorted her well maintained face.

Never mind. Never mind. I'll start over. First, is there someplace we can talk in private? I was getting impatient.

But I do not underztand. Are you not here to buy somezing?

No, not right now. It's about you and me.

You and me? But I do not even know you. I never zee you before in my life.

Okay, I said as I stepped closer to her. *Take a good look at my face. Don't tell me you don't see yourself in me. Well, I mean, on a bad hair day, that is. And don't count my outfit,* I added.

"Bad hair?" What iz...

Papers, I blurted out. *The papers. Do you have them?*

Damn. I should have gone in a little slower.

Too late.

Her eyes bulged out of their groomed little sockets, her face turned ashen and she ran to the back of the shop, knocking over a rack displaying two gold chain belted outfits waiting for a coupla' suckers to come along ready to pay full price. The rear office was cluttered with fabric swatches, plastic covered merchandise on hangers and tailoring accouterments ready to pin up the hem on the Rich Bitch getting all the attention out front. A heap of black and gold cardboard boxes toppled when I reached out for her leaving from the exit at the back of the office. The door led to a quiet alley where I was able to restrain her with a nifty arm hold I picked up from a former P.I. colleague back in California.

Please, I said as she twisted to break free. *I'm not going to hurt you. I'm on your side. I think. I just have to find out why you are being hunted down. Or why I am because they think I'm you. It doesn't matter. We both seem to be in some serious danger and since it's you they're after, I deserve to know why. Can we please talk?*

Who are you? What do you want wiz me? Pleaze leave me alone. I do not know anyzing about any paperz.

I was getting pissed off.

Look, I said through clenched teeth. *You, not me, are responsible for the trouble I'm in now.* Then I bugged out my eyes, teeth still clamped tight and took out my Cover Girl compact. I clasped her head next to mine, aimed it in the glass and continued, *Someone—someone I don't know, but you probably do, is after me. But it's not really me they are after. It's you. See? We look just alike. See?* I forced her to look again. *Get it? And I'm not leaving until you shed a little light on what the hell is going on. Comprend-o?*

The clenched teeth and bug eye bit worked.

Not here, she whispered. *Come wiz me.*

She took my hand and led me through the courtyard behind the shop. We headed down rue Duphot, a narrow street directly behind rue Cambon, eventually stopping in front of an elegant apartment building with wraparound balconies. Black and gold filigree railings held back enormous black lacquered pots filled with Kentia palms and Bird of Paradise trees.

Pinned inside a small pocket of her suit jacket was a gold ring holding three keys—an old fashioned front door key, a tiny one for a suitcase—or perhaps a secret diary, and another one that let us into a bright, spacious, airy penthouse apartment on the sixth floor. It was almost wall-to-wall windows with no coverings, ecru walls with white trim, pale ivory overstuffed sofas, chairs and ottomans, accented by huge sloppy pillows in Moroccan prints—bright purple, terra cotta, red, gold—some with jeweled trims or tassels. A tall Baccarat crystal vase filled with white orchids and gardenias sat in the middle of a impressive Chinese teak table supported by four massive carved legs the size of my thighs. It was an awesome room.

The sweet, tropical fragrance of plumeria permeating the air reminded me of one of the quiet places I often visit when I go off on one of my visualization trips. Yeah, this definitely could be a setting for one of my quiet places. I'll have to keep it in mind. I'll bet there's a gigantic walk-in closet so big that hanging items don't touch each other and stuff on shelves aren't piled so high that you need a step ladder every time you have to reach for a pair of sweats. *And* you never exit the closet with a unwanted T-shirt on your head or shoulder.

Zo, now we can talk, oui? She seemed to compose slightly once she was on her own turf.

Sure, I said, *but first, what's your name? Mine is Darra. Darra van Zandt.*

My name iz Marie-Louiz-ah. My surname iz not zo important. You do not need to know ziz information to talk wiz me.

Hmmm. I didn't appreciate the attitude of my evil twin, so I got to the crux of the situation *toot sweet:*

Okay, Marie-Louise, we'll leave it at that for now. Can you please enlighten me about some papers some people want to have real bad? And what do you know about some babies being born in a filthy warehouse not ten miles from here? And what about three men: Jacques, handsome and well-groomed, Henri, ugly and unkempt, and a drunken Arab doctor, name unknown.

Heh. Heh.

She became visibly shaken when I gave her the nasty facts in all of ten seconds. She reached for a slim sterling cigarette box on the teak table, taking one and motioning an offer to me. I was feeling more and more like I was getting into deep doo-doo, so somehow a cigarette, don't ask me why, seemed like just the ticket to calm me down. She lit both Gitanes with trembling hands and we simultaneously inhaled together, staring intently at each other's facial features. We exhaled at the same time.

She broke. *I am zo zorry zhat you have gotten involved in ziz, ziz, ziz horiblah, horiblah zituation. But you are right. You muzt know. You muzt know ze danger.*

Danger. That word again.

O-kaaay, I dragged out. *Go for it.*

Go for eet? What iz ziz "go for eet?"

Sorry. Please...ex-plain...fur-ther.... I articulated with exaggeration. This could get old fast.

She didn't pull any fancy tricks with her cigarette, just inhaled with feeling and tapped it out after three puffs. I did the same.

Ze three men you mention—Jacques Bertrand, Henri St-Jean, and Rahib Tahar—zhey are involved in a grande black market bébé zelling biznezz zhat iz run by a very dangerouz man by ze name of Mabouk. Zhese men, zhey take in runaway girlz, make zhem pregnant, sometimez wiz zheir own rot-tain sperm and keep zhem like animalz until it iz time for ze bébé to be born. Zhen zhey zend zhem away—ze new motherz. If ze girlz, if zhey are pretty, zheir tonguez are cut out and three fingerz of each hand and zhey are sent to Algeria to become ze sex slave of Mabouk. If zhey are really healthzey, and strong, zhey uze zhem for ze bébé over again. If zhey are lucky girlz...zhey are killed.

She was twisting her white linen handkerchief into a roll your own cigarette, so I handed her a real one out of her silver case and lit it for her. I joined her again.

Tears were streaming down her face as she continued. I unrolled her hanky and dabbed at her cheek. As she spoke, my own eyes welled up and I cried inside for the little girls I didn't help this morning.

Marie-Louise, how do you fit in? How can you be involved in this terrible scheme?, I said gently.

Then the waterworks came. She threw her head onto a betassled purple throw pillow and wailed for about three minutes until I came across a bottle of Napoleon Cognac, filled a crystal snifter from the wet bar, pulled her up and forced her to take a big gulp. She drained the glass before she started again.

Many yearz ago I waz ze very famouz runway model. Not only here in Pariz, but in all ze houses in Rome, Milan, London, New York. I waz, how you zay, very marketable when I waz still young and could go wiz out zo much cover of ze makeup. My life, it waz very buzy. Very exciting. Very wild. I lived on ze upperz, ze downerz, mari-juana, cham-pan-yay and little zleep. By ze time I waz of ze twenty-zeven yearz, my career as mannequin waz over. Fortunately, I met a very wonderful man—a man I did not dezerve. He waz much older zhan me, but much wizer, of courze, and he perzuaded me to give up all ze terriblah vices zhat were deztroying me. Even when he waz of fifty-three yearz and I waz of twenty-eight yearz, he wanted to have bébé wiz me. It would bring rezponzibility and stability to my life, he zaid.

We tried to have ze bébé for many yearz but we were alwayz wiz out luck. I had ze three mizcarriagez and each time ze doctor zay no, no, no, we muzt not try again. When I waz of thirty yearz my female tubez, zhey were damaged from, how you zay, ze pelvic diseaze, and ze doctor, he waz convinced it waz not pozzible for me to conceive and bring healthzey child to ziz world. For Antoine, my huzband, it waz important, but for me, it waz obzession. My entire life revolved around ze bébéz and ze void of not having one becauze of my own zelfish and deztructive behavior of ze past. We could not adopt becauze of Antoine's age. We tried ze invitro-fertilization two timez, but I became more and more dez-pon-dent each time it failed.

She blew her nose in the hanky, took a deep breath and continued…
Three yearz ago, I waz in hozpital for ze clinical depression. For two monthz I lived at Le Jardin Tranquille, just outzide ze city. It waz tres expenzive, catering to women wiz ze female problemz. Some patients were like me. Zhey didn't want to live if zhey could not have ze child. Antoine vizited often and I waz getting healthzier each day. Ze staff waz wonderful. Doctorz, nursez, and even ze Arabic women who cleaned and zerved uz our mealz. Malika, she waz like ze mama to

me. She would come in every morning at ten o'clock, walk wiz me to ze shade tree directly outside ze French doorz to my room and bring me a cup of tea while she made my room clean and cheerful. Alwayz ze fresh flowerz on ze table next to my bed. Alwayz ze fresh Algerian bread zhat she brought from home and sometimez even samsa, a North African paztry she brought for my tea in ze afternoon. When her work waz finizh, she would zit wiz me under ze tree and give me storiez about her country, Algeria—when she waz a young girl in Annaba, her home. I knew she had children, but she waz too kind to talk about them wiz me. She spoke only of her youth, her country, and how much she wanted to zee me happy again. She alwayz held my hand and squeezed it at ze precise moment she zaid "happy again".

Sometimez when Antoine came to vizit, I would be zleeping zo he would chat with Malika under ze shade tree until I woke up. He, too, thought she waz a beautiful person. I knew zhat I would mizz her very much when I went home again.

After I waz released from the clinic, I found ziz part time work at Chanel. After all, it waz my biznezz for many yearz and I found it helped to keep my mind off having ze child.

I waz doing much better, but Antoine knew zhat ze treatment did only az much az it ever could do to help me cope wiz my pain. Only to cope. Nothzing more.

One day—two yearz ago tomorrow, I waz zleeping late on a Monday morning. I do not work on Monday. Antoine had been away zince Thurzday—a biznezz meeting in Marseilles. I waz awakened by ze sound of ze front door opening and ze quiet footzteps of zomeone walking towardz our bedroom.

It waz Antoine. He looked very tired and troubled. He had a white package in hiz armz. Wiz tearz in hiz eyes, he came to me, and wiz out speaking, bent down and placed ze package along zide of me in my bed. My daughter, Angelique, only a few hourz old, waz in her mamaz armz for ze first time.

I waz crazy wiz happinezz and fear and sadnezz at ze same time. I did not want to question Antoine. I waz afraid to question Antoine. Angelique waz ourz and she waz ourz to stay. I did not want to know anymore zhan zhat. When Antoine ztarted to speak I quieted him wiz a finger to hiz lips and it waz never brought up again, until...until...

She cracked again.

Do you want another brandy? I asked as I poured a jigger for myself. *Oui, oui, merci.*

I looked at the Art Deco marble clock on the fireplace mantle and started to worry about the time. It was three o'clock and there were still so many unanswered questions. I was toying with the idea of involving the French police, probably the smart thing to do based on my past track record in crime solving, but I wanted to know more first.

Try to go on, Marie-Louise. It's very important.

She took a large, unladylike sip of brandy. So did I.

Two monthz ago, on ze Friday afternoon, Antoine called to tell me zhat he would be late coming home and perhapz it would not be until ze next day az he had to take a flight to Marseilles for biznezz. He haz done zhat often enough zo I did not think it strange. He told me how much he loved me and our Angelique and promized to take uz to ze country on ze weekend for ze lovely picnic.

He never...Antoine...he never came home. Hiz car waz found at Orly airport. It waz parked in ze long term parking lot and hiz attaché case and set of keyz were found in ze trunk.

And ze police, ze police were not very helpful. Zhey tried to pazz it off az only a Frenchman viziting hiz miztress for ze weekend, az many Frenchmen do ziz. I waz certain Antoine did not have a miztress but most women will zay ze zame. I became curiouz and decided to look around hiz study to see if zhere waz any evidence to hold up ze miztress theory of ze French police.

When I waz tired from looking, I clozed ze heavy side drawer of hiz desk but while doing zo I found a secret compartment underneath it. It waz jammed. Impozzible to cloze. I took a knife and opened it.

Inzide ze secret drawer were paperz—paperz zhat had no meaning for me. Zhey were...zhey were...

Stop, Marie-Louise, I said. *The papers. Were these papers birth certificates?*

Oui, oui, oui, mais, how do you know ziz?

I don't have time to explain now, Marie-Louise. Go on about the birth certificates. I didn't mean to interrupt. Sorry. Go on, please.

Birth certificatez and pazzportz az well, she said as she got up and walked around the room. She paced back and forth, then stopped, faced the window looking out on the rue Cambon. With her back to me—just like they do on soap operas—she continued...

On Angelique's firzt birzday, our zelebration for her waz interrupted by an urgent phone call for my huzband. Zhese callz were becoming more and more frequent. When he returned to ze party, he waz upzet and zaid he had to leave immediately for ze important meeting. I did not zee him until ze next night. Very late. Very late. It waz midnight, at least. I waz azleep but I felt my husband watching me and when I opened my eyez, he waz looking at me with such dezpair and zorrow on his face. I inztantly thought of Angelique. It waz not until I could go to her myzelf to see zhat she waz safely azleep in ze nursery zhat I could relax. When I returned, Antoine and I zat across from each othzer on ze bed and he poured out hiz heart to me.

Another cig. Another slug of brandy......

While I waz still in clinic, Antoine had made ze many long converzations with Malika about how dezperately we wanted a child. It waz just before I waz releazed zhat Malika phoned him at hiz office and asked to meet him zomewhere away from ze clinic. He waz curiouz zo he met her at a café in ze 18th Arrondissement, ze Café de l'Afrique. She iz telling him how much she cared for uz both and how sad she waz to zee me zo unhappy. She knew zomeone who could help uz, she zaid. She gave Antoine a phone number, embraced him and left ze bar quickly wiz out offering any othzer information.

Antoine did not want to zay anything to me becauze of my fragile mental condition. After waiting three dayz, he called ze number and went on hiz own for an appointment wiz Mabouk. To Antoine, Mabouk appeared to be a diztinguished biznezz man but mostly he showed ze compassion for our predicament and wanted to truly help uz. He had only one condition...

Her voice broke when she murmured "condition". Crumbling under the strain of having to reveal the dark family secret, she stopped and stared out the window for a full minute. I took advantage of the pause to relight my dead cigarette and fill up her snifter. I walked over to her back, handed the glass over her shoulder and she went on...

Antoine iz working for ze Mairie—how you zay in English, ze City Hall, of ze 1st Arrondissement for zhirty-five yearz. He waz very young when he started working for ze government zo he became familiar with every azpect of how official documents were issued; he himzelf worked in Pazzport issuance and birth records in ze very early days. He iz highly regarded, trusted implicitly and zherefore haz free accezz to all departmentz at all timez, day or night. No one would ever question ze credibility of my Antoine. Somehow—ziz man— Mabouk, he knew ziz about my huzband. At first zhey only wanted him to repay zhem for our Angelique by providing one official birth document and ze pazzport for one child. Zhey needed to take ze child to anothzer country. Zhey did not say where, just zhat zhey needed proper documentation to get him into ze country.

She turned around, walked back over to the sofa where I was sitting and in a slow motion zombie like fashion, sat down next to me. Gazing straight ahead, she spoke more softly now—almost in a whisper—as if her shame could not bear to hear her own voice utter the rest of the story:

Antoine knew...he knew he waz making a deal wiz ze devil, but he did it anyway.

More tears.

*He provided ze paperz zhey wanted. But zhen zhey called on him again. And he did it again, and again, and again...*She faded off.

I've never been a touchy-feely kind of woman but I was so taken by her story that I found my two earthy hands embracing her manicured left one with genuine compassion. I patted and squeezed it a few times until she was composed and could continue to speak through guilty tears:

Even zo our life with Angelique waz happy, I could zee zhat ziz sacrifice Antoine made to give uz a child waz making him very, very sick. In hiz head. In hiz heart. He lost very much weight and seemed to grow old overnight.

Zhen he dizappeared. I told you I implored upon ze Police to help me and zhey took a report, and zaid zhey would investigate, but I do not believe zhat zhey work zo much on ziz case. Every time I call ze Inspector Clement, ze police inzpector assigned to our case, he tellz me he iz still working hard, but nothzing, nothzing do I hear more.

*Zhen...five days ago, Malika came here to our flat to speak wiz me. She waz very upzet, crying and wringing her hands az she told me zhat Mabouk, ze leader of ziz organization, ze **la vente d'enfants au marcher noir**—zhat iz, a black market baby zelling operation, had ordered Antoine silenzed becauze he had refused to be a part of zheir evil enterprize any longer.*

She zaid zhat zhey were convinced zhat I knew everyzhing and zhat zhey were waiting for me to provide ze next three setz of documents. She zaid ze paperz muzt be in zheir hands by Zaturday.

Uh, that's today. Today is Zaturday, er....Saturday, Marie-Louise, I said shaking her hand away from its comfort station.

Do you mean today, Saturday, or next week Saturday? You mean next week Saturday, right?

Non, today Zaturday. Ze 2nd of April. Oui, it iz today, Zaturday.

Well, uh, then, Marie-Louise, can I ask you this? Do you have the papers? And if so, what are we, I mean you, going to do with them? We, I mean you, cannot let these creeps continue to destroy young girl's lives by making them baby machines and then discarding them like a dirty diaper, I said using an inappropriate use of words, I admit. *Do you have any idea what really happens to these girls, Marie-Louise?,* I ranted. *Unfortunately, I do. I saw it just this morning. I saw a girl child giving birth and two more ready to deliver as well. Don't make me describe the squalid conditions, Marie-Louise. You couldn't handle it, trust me.*

She was sobbing again and I was getting a maternal surge. I held on to her shoulders, forced eye contact and spoke evenly:

Marie-Louise, I know what you must have felt when you received Angelique. She was a gift from God, right? Wrong, Marie-Louise. She was not God's gift. It was a gift with strings attached. God doesn't tie strings to His blessings. But I don't think He's gonna pass judgment on you today. What we hafta' do is stop the atrocities happening right now, as we speak. Now, Marie-Louise! Don't let it go on one more day. We hafta' do something now. We can't just sweep it under your fancy Persian rug here. You have your Angelique, but your husband has paid dearly for it.

I was really roughing her up but I couldn't help it…it just poured out and it turned out to be effective.

Now, I said, *where is your daughter? Where is Angelique?*

Angelique iz safe with Malika. I let her take my daughter wiz her. I waz concerned for her zafety—zhat zhey may try to take her away if I didn't cooperate zo she iz wiz Malika.

Okay. And what about this Malika? How do you know if she is a good guy or bad guy? How do we know she didn't set you up in the first place?

Oh, no. You do not underztand our relationzhip with Malika. She iz alwayz only wanting ze best for uz. She lovez uz very much and we her.

I recalled the towheaded babe sleeping next to the middle aged woman at the warehouse but didn't want to start putting ideas in her head. I kept my second hunch to myself and said,

Fine. Do you mind if I use the toilet and then we can work out what to do next.

Notice how I say, "toilet." If you tell someone in Europe that you have to go to the "bathroom," they assume you want to take a bath. She directed me down the hall, second door on the left.

I did have to go to the bathroom but I also wanted an excuse to pry around a bit on my way. First door on the left was closed. I pretended like I misunderstood the directions and opened it. Nursery. Pink. Ruffles. Lace. Empty. A large framed Picasso print I proudly recognized as "Mère et Enfant", hung on the otherwise bare wall.

The second door on the left was indeed the toilet room. Except that the money put into this room was probably more than my entire house in Podunk, Holland is worth. Including land. It didn't look like a toilet room. It looked more like a miniature Hearst Castle that just happened to have a toilet in it. The bathtub was vanilla veined black Italian marble. Solid gold fixtures featured playful golden dolphin water spouts with two baby dophinettes posed to spew hot or cold water with a twist of their golden tails. There was a massive skylight overhead, providing the perfect light for the ferns and wild orchids hanging at different levels from the high ceiling. A creamy satin chaise longue loaded up with black and cream print pillows perched three steps up in a glorious alcove—an area officially set apart for changing but it was—no lie, big enough to throw a party in. Two fluffy robes—one white, one black, hung on golden hooks. Tons of bottles of perfume, not sample flacons like I use, lined up on the inch thick glass dressing table. Above the table hung a fabulously tall bevelled mirror from the thirties. Just the right size for full body primping.

Normally I would check myself out in any mirror, but somehow it didn't appeal to me at the moment. To be honest, I knew what I'd see and after pretending to look in every way like Marie-Louise for the last half hour, I wasn't ready to give up the fantasy just yet. However, there *was* a simple digital weigh scale sitting innocently next to the door and I'll be doggoned if I didn't have to get on it to see how I was doing this week. Hmmmm, not bad. I lost a kilo—that's 2.2 U.S. pounds, in the last three days, and that's *with* clothes on and a full stomach. When I stepped off, it made an embarrassing *beep-beep-beep* noise that alerted anyone within hearing distance that I just weighed myself. I coughed during the second and third beeps hoping to cause a distraction. What a stupid machine, I thought.

The phone was going on its fourth ring when I reached the end of the hall to rejoin Marie-Louise.

Allo, oui? Oui, c'est Madame Trudeau. Qui est à l'appareil?

Non, non, non, she cried out before she collapsed on the fancy Persian rug.

I picked up the receiver and said *"allo, oui?"* but the line was dead. I wet her white linen handkerchief in the ice bucket and dabbed her forehead until she came to.

She came to then she screamed.

Ten

Two minutes later Marie-Louise was coherent enough to give me the details of the call.

Ce n'est pas possible. Pas possible. Angelique, she iz wiz Malika, she cried, trying to convince herself.

Marie-Louise, Marie-Louise, Look at me!, I said with uncharacteristic authority in my voice.

Look at me, Marie-Louise, gently shaking her shoulders to make her focus. *What did the caller say? Was it a man, woman, what?*

Man. It waz...Mabouk.

Exactly what did Mabouk say, Marie-Louise?

He zay, I must bring paperz to Café de l'Afrique at five o'clock today. If I do not follow hiz instruction, my Angelique will go away from me

80

forever. Oh, non, non, I cannot bear to lose alzo my Angelique, my angel.

Okay, Marie-Louise. Here's what we do. Now, first you have to calm down no matter how frightened you are.

I meant how frightened "we" are but didn't want to send her off the deep end. She was depending on me to save her soul, rescue Angelique, find her husband safe and sound, shut down the sordid baby business and God knows what else.

Little did she know.

I want to call the Police, Marie-Louise.

Non, non, non. Mabouk, he zay no police or I will regret.

Oh, Lordy.

Okay, where are the papers?

She took out the small key she had pinned to her black jacket, hurried into the study and returned with a heavy metal lock box. Inside were three incomplete birth certificates printed on watermarked parchment. The spaces to indicate male or female were still blank, but a special government rubber stamp bearing an official seal, a purple inked stamp pad and a weird sort of pen, obviously specially designed to certify documents, were neatly arranged in another compartment within the metal box. Three passports, requiring the same sort of authentication were tucked under the certificates.

Marie-Louise and I looked at each other for a moment in communication—but without speaking. We were two mothers in trouble. We both wanted to see our children again. We were afraid we wouldn't. Our two sets of look alike hazel eyes said all that without making a sound.

My mind sailed off in the direction of California. I wondered if Christian had gotten my message on his answer machine. What if the message I left from the hotel was the last time he would ever hear my voice? What if he didn't know that and erased the tape before he did know it? And if he did know it, would he still erase it eventually? Or would he keep it forever to remember me by? Or would he use it again because he didn't have a spare cassette to use the next time he had to leave the house and was waiting for a call from some guy to go fishing because Rock Cod were biting heavy duty off Catalina.

I didn't know where her head went but when a poor woe-be-gone expression slowly formed on her face I knew that I would have to forge ahead and take total fake control.

I looked up to the ceiling and quietly whispered, *Dear Friend, please tell me what to do. Thank You.* I learned long ago that prayers don't need to be long and flowery—just sincere.

Okay, here's the plan. I made up as I went along. *You, Marie-Louise are much too upset to go to this café and meet Mabouk. I'll go. We look alike for sure, but with a little spit and polish...*

What iz ziz "zpit and polizh" thing you zay, she screamed hysterically. She was losing it.

Again I question why the whole world doesn't speak one language. I mean it. It causes so much miscommunication between people, not to mention aggravation.

Ne-ver mind. Take me to your bed-room.

She clutched my arm and practically dragged me back down the hall to a room facing rue Duphot. The large master bedroom had french doors leading out to a spacious red tiled balcony. Tall palms in round black pots were situated on each side for privacy between flats and a white bistro table was set up for morning latte and croissants.

This room was also in many shades of white with splashes here and there of bold North African prints. And sure enough. Closets big enough to live in. No lie. One was as big as my daughter's bedroom. She must have had twenty or thirty Chanel suits, twelve jackets with skirts, umpteen silk blouses hanging inches apart on padded pink satin hangers. They hung in color order—a fashion rainbow of sorts. An ocean of shoes in the same shades stood very orderly on specially made shoe shelves with their unscuffed noses facing closet visitors. I had to do a jealous chuckle when I thought of the matchbox I call a closet at home in Holland.

We had a good hour and a half before I had the meeting at Café de l'Afrique. I needed all the time I could get if I was going to pass as Marie-Louise. I tried to shoo her out, suggesting that she put together some clothes for Angelique for when we picked her up, but she was out of it. She just sat on a bistro chair on the balcony weeping and intermittently murmuring, *Angelique...Antoine...Angelique............ ...Antoine.*

I had to carry on. First stop: Hair. I didn't have time to wallow luxuriously in that big black bathtub, but the shower wasn't bad. Quite a trip actually. The skylight extending over the shower was totally open. The stall was so large that it didn't even need a shower curtain that could stick to your butt. It felt like I was outside. Rather naughty. Rather adventurous. I washed my hair with shampoo out of an elegant crystal bottle, a few pearls floating around near the bottom. I couldn't figure out if they were real pearls—and if so, for what reason, or if they were "shampoo" pearls that burst open every now and then inside the bottle to add even more silkiness to the already ultra rich suds. A matching essence of pearl conditioner, which of course I always need to control unruly frizz, insured a successful hair repair.

I used the white terrycloth robe hanging in the alcove party room and towel dried my hair. Marie-Louise was much more composed when I got back to the bedroom, but a quick P.I. observation revealed an open bottle of some prescription drug sitting on her night table. My guess would be Valium or a close cousin. She looked a little glassy eyed and with good reason. With the amount of cognac she just drank in combination with how ever many tranquilizers she just swallowed, I figured that I'd be dealing with a total rag doll in about five more minutes.

Marie-Louise, dear,... I started to patronize her, *how about going to the kitchen to make us a nice cup of coffee before we go? Do you have an espresso machine? Perhaps we could have a couple of cups before we leave, okay, Marie-Louise? That would be nice, don't you think, dear? Please, go to kitchen now. Make coffee.* I enunciated every word as if I were talking to Christina when she was three years old.

She didn't say anything as she made a careful slo-mo turn and shuffled toward the kitchen.

I presumed that Marie-Louise would not be quibbling over which outfit I chose to wear to pass for her, so I took the liberty of selecting my favorite—the Jackie Kennedy pink and black ensemble she wore yesterday. I assembled it across the bed with one jacket sleeve in a waving-to-a-crowd position while the other was folder over to depict a hand on hip attitude. I know this sounds sick, but I was really getting off on all this richness and glamour business. I looked at the future me sprawled out on the bed, closed my eyes to visualize the transformation which included my size 12"ish" self compressing to fit the Chanel size 8.

I slipped the slim skirt over my hips, sucked in as I struggled to button the waistband, which unfortunately was not elastic, and did the same with the jingle jangley jacket. It worked. I was in it. I was delighted.

My hair came out absolutely great. Under other circumstances I would have asked to take a bit of her shampoo and conditioner home in an empty jelly jar or something, but the time wasn't right.

I sampled almost every Germaine Monteil make-up aid she had on her dressing table. Eye firmer (Aha!), concealer (Aha! again), Honey Bisque foundation and loose powder, Passionate Plum eyeliner, Burnt Sienna blusher, Sandy Sable eyebrow and mole filler and Oh! So Noir black mascara. I lined my lips for the first time, hopefully not as dramatically as Madame Bouchet, and filled in with Pink Piquant out of a little silver pot. There wasn't much hope for my hands and nails, but I toned down the workman look the best I could by stroking a thin coat of Romantic Rose lacquer on my ten stubs.

There was a satin lined hosiery drawer next to the organized shoe department. Each pair was protected in individual pink satin pouches—I snickered at the opulence some people live in—and chose a ultra sheer black. I found the matching shoes—soft black leather pumps with a very thin pink border around the rim and heel. They were a nine. I wear a ten. I made them work.

The Art Deco mirror was waiting for me in the bathroom.

Tum dee dee dum....

Wow, do I ever wash up nice, I thought and then said out loud cause I was the only one there.

Ummmm....I smelled coffee.

It had been a while since I thought about Marie-Louise. I was really getting caught up in this make-over experience when the aroma of coffee and a suspicious noise coming from the direction of the kitchen snapped me out of the lovin' myself trance. I ran to the kitchen to find Marie-Louise busy making espresso for twenty people. There were six cups on the counter, some over-turned, some full, and much more streaming out of Mr. Espresso onto the hardwood floor. Marie-Louise was holding herself up with one elbow on the counter top, but when she saw me—her rescuer, her Rock of Gibraltar, she gave up and crumpled to the floor.

I took a copper saucepan off a hook and put it under the machine to collect the excess coffee, dragged Marie-Louise away from the growing puddle on the floor—being careful not to muss my outfit— and propped her up on the padded breakfast nook bench. I filled two cups out of the copper pot, moved her against the wall and sat closely next to her for support.

Here, drink this, Marie-Louise. Mar-ie-Lou-is-e, drink this coffee and it will make you feel better, I fibbed. *Come on' now, drink up like a good girl. We have to be strong, Marie-Louise, remember? We have to find An-gel-ique, don't we?,* I said, emphasizing the child's name.

Bingo. The sound of Angelique's name made Marie-Louise shoot straight up in the chair. She still looked dopey, but she was able to drink down her coffee as well as mine before she got that pathetic, pleading look in her eyes again.

I was really feeling a heavy burden had been placed on my shoulders but I knew there was no way of walking away now. I just wish that my sidekick was a little more dependable, that's all.

I forced her to talk for a while to wake her up. She told me all she knew about Mabouk. She only knew what Antoine had told her, which was that he was around fifty years old, was half French and half Algerian, spoke Arabic, flawless French and English and was an extremely ruthless, cunning and dangerous human being.

Well, now, that's good to know, I thought. Gives me a good base to work with. Shrewd, no-conscience, diabolic low-life meets insecure American/Dutch housewife on foreign soil to make blackmail exchange. Should be no problem-o.

Marie-Louise was coming around. We had a half hour before we had to meet my date at Café de l'Afrique, a fifteen minute ride away, so I asked her not to disturb me for at least seven minutes and dashed off to her bedroom. I threw off the killer black Jackie-O shoes, spread out on the white satin coverlet, closed my eyes, and took three deep breaths. My body went limp after the third inhalation, leading me into my Alpha level of consciousness and my quiet place.

My quiet place is along a blue Mediterranean coastline, gentle waves lapping up against a white sandy beach. My slender, golden body is barely covered by a pink and black thong bikini, a slave chain belt with double crossed "C's" holding it together, hung loosely from my almost non-existent hips and flat stomach. With no pressing appointments in my agenda, I am resting peacefully in a white braided hammock tied around two swaying palm trees—the breezes moving to and fro through my well conditioned hair. I am sipping on a Trinidad Rum Punch and snacking on no calorie potato chips. A little lady, short dark hair with bangs answering to "Coco", comes out of my white Spanish villa to tell me she is through organizing my wardrobe and is there anything else she can do for me. Anything. No, I say, just come back tomorrow when I have to get dressed and do it for me. My trustworthy Arabic man servant, a former convicted murderer turned reborn Christian, is fanning me with gigantic peacock plumes. He, as well as everyone who has ever known or even met me, has great respect and admiration for my honesty, compassion, and most of all, the courage and confidence to overcome every adversity in life. I feel completely relaxed. Completely rested. Completely confident. I feel invincible. I am invincible. I am anxious for the next challenge in my life to present itself so I can conquer it with total conviction that the outcome will be for the betterment of all mankind.

I affirm how much I love myself unconditionally three times, take three deep breaths, stretch my arms over my head, leave the Alpha and return to the Beta level of consciousness.

I was so completely relaxed that with my last deep breath I slithered off the satin bed cover and on to the thick, cushy ecru carpet. I know it seems like a luxury to go off on these side trips, but they are necessary, I truly believe it. Now, where was I? Eight minutes have past and I'm feeling better. I stuffed my feet back into the Cinderella slippers, took them off again and slipped into my own comfortable black flats. I decided that if my black flats turned out to be a dead give-away that I'm not the former famous model, Marie-Louise Trudeau, well then, I'd just have to deal with it when the time comes.

Poor Marie-Louise. I left her alone for eight minutes and came back to find her snoozing on the sofa. I guess the combination of drugs, alcohol and espresso were too much for her system because it appears that just before nodding off she got rid of her breakfast all over the shiny teak coffee table.

I looked at the hopeless sight before me and begrudgingly accepted the fact that I was going to have to go off on this drop alone. I was hoping that Marie-Louise would at least be able to drive me to Café de l'Afrique—wherever the hell it was, hide down the street, and maybe call the police if I didn't come out in twenty minutes. A little back-up would have been nice.

Against Mabouk's explicit instruction, I put a call in to this here "Inspector Clement" at the 1st Arrondissement Paris Police precinct.

He was just leaving for the day but I was able to convince him that I had a sound lead on the disappearance of Antoine Trudeau and we had to meet. I was taking a big chance, but I told him to meet me at Café de l'Afrique at six o' clock, just after my meeting with Mabouk. For obviously reasons I insisted that he allow me to approach him rather than him me and he agreed, giving me a brief description of himself:

Blond. Big. Raincoat.

Ummm, I can't wait.

I collected the birth certificates, passports, official stamp, pad and ink pen from the large metal box, put them in an empty leather attaché case I found in the study, patted Marie-Louise compassionately on the head, left the upchuck on the coffee table and hurried downstairs to flag down a taxicab.

It was 4:45 by my borrowed Piaget wristwatch.

My North African cab driver was familiar with the Belleville area of Eastern Paris where I was to meet Mabouk so he whisked me there in less than fifteen minutes. He dropped me off right in front of my meeting point, which was a dingy café sitting caddy corner from a street market closing down for the day. Old cabbage heads, splattered tomatoes, overripe melons and empty couscous and lamb kebab paper cups were strewn a block long. Street cleaners in blue overalls shuffled through the rubble with twig brooms. The long sweeping strokes seemed to keep rhythm with the Algerian pop music drifting from the restaurant below the hotel on the opposite corner.

I walked into Café de l'Afrique at precisely 5:00 PM. I was relieved that I was not going to have to sit and get more nervous waiting if I had been any earlier. It took a couple of minutes to adjust my eyes to the seven watt lighting around the room. I sat down at a table for two close to the door. Lighted candles stuck in Beaujolais wine bottles were used to add ambiance to the dungeon like atmosphere but it only made me feel as if I sat in a hellish waiting room—my appointment with Dr. Devil now five minutes late.

It was 5:05 PM.

A geriatric bartender with a bald head and bag o' bones body saw me as I walked in but chose not to wait on me. It didn't matter. I wasn't sure what was safe to drink in this joint, anyway. I sat facing the door so I could see Mabouk when he came in. I didn't know what he looked like but I was sure he would be at least 6'2", 210, broad shoulders—built like a bull, wiry gray hair, bulbous nose, eyes like a weasel, flashy white teeth against cocoa skin, black sharkskin suit, Rolex watch and maybe a ruby ring on his left hand that he forces his slaves to bow to and kiss every day.

It was 5:10.

The door opened sending a shock of light into the dark den. A couple, an American couple—I looked down at their shoes—stumbled in as if they were lost—a good guess based on the character of this dump and the expressions on their faces. They sat down anyway, sure enough right next to me, and I welcomed the diversion.

Hi there, she greeted me. *DO-YOU-SPEAK-ENGLISH-I-O?* She said with a raised voice.

Why, yes, yes I do. I am American. Are you guys lost or what?

Oh, Heavens to Betsy, nawww. Lloyd and I jes' wanna 'sperience a lil' ethnic color of Paris, that's all. We've been sightseein' till its comin' outta our ears—Notra Daime, the See-ne River cruise, the Moo-len Rooge, and we jes got back from a half day sightseein' bus tour 'round the city. It was grreaat, wadn't it, Lloyd, honey? That sightseein' tour we jes took. It was grreat, wadn't it?

Lloyd wasn't paying much attention to his wife and her new friend. He was busy ordering mixers of Diet Coke and Schweppes Tonic Water with extra, extra ice to compliment the Bacardi and Beefeater miniatures he had just unscrewed under the table and left hidden on the empty chair in the corner next to him. When a young Tunisian girl placed the bottles of mixers and glasses, each containing a solo ice cube on the table, Lloyd looked up, smiled sheepishly and said, *Gee, thanks, Madomosell. You're a doll. We are just soooo thirsty and nothin' works better than a nice cool Coke, I always say. Ummmmm. Ya know what I mean? In't that right, Cora?* Instead of a mere thank you, his elaboration condemned him guilty of something, poor bloke.

I felt funny about being a witness to their crime in progress, so I took an extra long time to check my watch, count the hundreds of used lotto tickets on the floor as well as the number of missing linoleum tiles while he poured the contents of the little bottles into their glasses. Cora stood guard while he did it. With the deed done, and relief on their faces, they lifted their glasses in a toast either to their health or in celebration of getting away with yet another cheap drink caper, and took big swigs.

It was 5:20 and no one resembling a demonic tyrant had come in or out of Café de l'Afrique since I walked in precisely at 5:00 o'clock. I double checked the name of the place with an empty matchbook in the ashtray, leaned back on my chair, nestled the attaché to my chest and ordered a bottle of beer from the passing waitress.

Cora and Lloyd were a cutesy couple in their sixties who have been together so long that they were in perfect sync with each other. Everything she started, he finished, and vice versa. He started counting out francs and she finished the count. She took out her compact to touch up her nose and he clicked it closed and zipped it away in her shoulder bag. He ordered another Diet Coke and Tonic this time with *extra, extra, extra* ice and she unscrewed two new mini-bottles of booze and held them posed under the table.

Cora had a face that couldn't hide disappointment. When the girl brought their mixers over with yet again one lonely ice cube floating around in each glass, Cora's forehead crinkled and she let out a discouraged sigh. Lloyd was just happy to have another drink—*ice, schmice,* I heard him mutter.

I was so nervous I couldn't even fully enjoy my favorite pastime. I turned away from my fellow Americans and stared straight at the door.

I gave Mabouk fifteen more minutes.

At 5:35 Cora and Lloyd paid their very reasonable tab, Cora told me how much she *luvved* my outfit and they walked out in unison. Four empty plastic bottles tumbled to the floor behind them.

I got up to leave. Time was up for this Mabouk character, I said to myself. I put my hand on the door handle to give it a pull and out of nowhere a callused, prune-like hand grabbed my wrist.

*D*a paperz, a rough voice demanded. *Gif me everyting now. At once!*

I was looking straight ahead, afraid to face this Mabouk monster, but when I finally did, it was only the harmless old bartender.

Ohmygod.

He yanked the case away from me, threw his apron across the bar and was gone. He had obviously been waiting for Cora and Lloyd to leave before he could approach me.

After the initial panic passed I ran outside to see if I could catch his direction but he was long gone. And a good thing, too. When I turned around to head back into the café to wait for Inspector Clement, I ran smack dab into Marie-Louise, looking like I used to look—mascara running down her face, hairdo askew, runs in her silk stockings, and she didn't smell all that fresh either. A bit throw-uppy.

Marie-Louise, what in the hell are you doing here? I can't believe it. What you are doing here? You know you just missed running into Mabouk, don'tcha? What's gotten into you? And how did you get here?

Where iz Angelique? Where iz my bébé? She screamed in my face.

I looked around and saw that she had driven her silver Citroën XM up on the curb. She had side-swiped a lamppost, the driver's side door wide open.

Oh damn, Marie-Louise, did you drive over here in this condition? Gimme those keys. Give. Me. The. Keys.

I had to wrestle the car keys away from her and push her into the café to discourage the crowd forming out on the sidewalk. I guided her over to a dark booth in the back of the bar and ordered a double Moroccan coffee for her—the kind you can slice with a knife—and hoped it would do the trick. I sipped on my warm Kronenburg while I mentally prepared my speech to her about how the papers were gone, Angelique still was, and that I called the police against the blackmailer's wishes.

Marie-Louise, everything is under control. I chickened out. *Everything is going according to plan so why don't you just sit her for awhile until you pull yourself together then drive home carefully. I promise to call or come over the very second I have good news for you.*

I gave her the most convincing face I could summon up from my facial expression repertoire and hoped that she'd buy it.

Non, non, non.

In French that means I don't buy it. She held on to my pink jacket looking as if she was about to say something profound, but she lost her train of thought and dropped her head to the table. My heart was going out to this anguished woman and I wanted so desperately to fix

93

up her life but mine was not exactly in divine order at the moment either.

The bar door opened at precisely 6:00 P.M. and in walked Inspector Philippe Clement. It had to be him and yet he looked so unlike a cop. His blonde hair was shiny, wavy and shoulder length; unevenly parted down the middle. His nose was long, slightly crooked and squashed from a prior encounter with either a fist or baseball bat. He was at least 6' 3" and built like a Mack truck but it was more natural than Nautilus. His raincoat fitted him like a lycra bodysuit. It was probably too small for me even. I had to laugh at the total package but after I laughed I got a lump in my throat when our eyes met. The moment he walked in the room I got the same feeling I had when I came across those two brown rats earlier today. I got the feeling that this Inspector Clement was one of those Angels-come-down-to-earth-to-rescue-and-at-the-same-teach-a-lesson-to beings.

And I was totally smitten.

Halo....I mean hello, you must be Inspector Clement.

Yes, that is correct. And you are?...

Oh, sorry, I am Darra van Zandt posing as Marie-Louise Trudeau and this is, I believe you've met...this is Marie-Louise Trudeau, pointing to the disheveled head of hair on the table.

His heavenly blue green eyes got a real confused look in them right off the bat. I was going to have to fill him in on everything that had transpired since I fell into this adventure, but we were going to have to do it on the way to where I thought Mabouk was headed.

Fortunately, Inspector Clement had ordered back-up to wait across the street unless it became necessary to assist, so when we walked outside the bar he signaled an officer to take over with Marie-Louise—either to let her sleep it off at the table or struggle with her to get her home. I was secretly happy that I was not going to have to be there when she came round again to find out that Angelique was not there—not safe yet. My credibility with her was weakening, so perhaps a French speaking person, like this Officer Goulet, would be more comforting.

Inspector Clement didn't question me or give me a hard time. I told him we had to be somewhere fast and he just followed my lead. Although, once we were in his unmarked police car, he started quizzing me: Who was I really; what was I doing here; what do I know about the disappearance of Antoine Trudeau; and last, where was I taking him.

I told him everything I knew except the last part because I wasn't even sure. It had only been a few hours, so luckily my short term memory served me well enough when it came down to which highway to take out of town and the landmarks leading to the warehouse. But the dirt road I ran down to get to the two-lane highway was nowhere in sight. We double backed a few times. Nothing seemed familiar anymore. On the third try back we saw a long black limousine, pulling a trailer, squeal out from one of the unpaved roads on the right. It fishtailed on to the highway leaving a huge brown cloud of dust behind it.

Now here's the part where I always seem to screw up:

That's it, I cried. *That's the road. Turn here. Turn right. No, go straight, follow that limo. Oh, no. Oh, God, I just don't know.*

Fast decision making has never been my forté.

We couldn't be certain that the black limo was affiliated with the Mabouk Group, so at my insistence, we made a mutual decision to turn right. He turned right on to the dirt road and instantly I knew this place. I could almost see a heavy, foreboding shroud of gloom hovering over it that could compare with the brown gray color of a maximum Smog Alert day in downtown Los Angeles. The rusty metal sign we had to drive under swung precariously from a rotten beam and told us that we were entering the property of *Pétrole d'Or de France*, an abandoned oil surplus depository.

On the way to the warehouse, I convinced the inspector that I was not just a hysterical American housewife with a vivid imagination but that I recently retired as a very highly respected private investigator in my own country. I'm gettin' good. I almost believed my own lie. I mean, I couldn't tell him the truth could I? That I was a comedic version of any one of the Charlie's Angels—preferably Farrah Fawcett. I boldly told him he could run a check on me but of course I was bluffing. It was an easy bluff because I knew that time was of the essence and he needed me to lead him to Mabouk. The deeper I got into this escapade, however, the more I did wish I was just a housewife who would soon be waking up after a night of wild dreams. I would get up, go through my morning breakfast ritual and get safely lost in the latest episode of As The World Turns.

Just barely into the yard, we spotted a dilapidated shed wide enough to conceal his little Peugeot. We backed in, hid the car, then quietly got out to find the warehouse where I had spent last night.

I was trying to fight the attraction I had for Inspector Clement—or Phillipe, as I knew I would be calling him eventually. I was sure it would go no further, or so the rational department of my psyche was trying to convince the emotional sector. Truth be known, I was indeed lusting after him in my heart. He looked to be in his early forties, clean cut, and radiated extreme self-confidence even before he spoke. Within minutes of our acquaintance I could sense a healthy awareness and appreciation of spirit, of soul, of heart, of life, of everything good and righteous.

A clear cut case of opposites attracting.

He spoke almost perfect American English—nothing ornate, just plain ol' abusive to the King of England: wanna,' gonna,' getta' American. He explained that he left France at eighteen to go to school in the U.S. He ended up staying for fifteen years when he married and settled down in upstate New York. That's all we got during the twenty minute drive to the warehouse. I wasn't able to fish out his current marital status, but as per typical of how my mind works, I guessed he was still unhappily tied down to some East Coast bimbo who probably tricked him into marriage via the old "I didn't get my friend this month" ploy.

We moved quickly through the rows and rows of empty oil barrels and cable reels, stopping at every fifty yard intersection to check for enemy traffic. I really was unsure about just how far into this compound we should look. It was a whole lot bigger than I remembered, but I must say I was impressed with how much I did recall considering the consequences that brought me here the night before. I had been carrying around a Mai-Tai size headache since opening my eyes this morning so I continued to amaze myself with some of the correct moves I'd made thus far today.

In ten minutes we reached a row of buildings but they all looked exactly the same. We began with the closest, sneaking up along the corrugated siding to find any sort of opening—window, door, crack. It appeared that all the buildings were uniform: the main loading dock door was practically the entire width of the hundred foot wide building, one small door on the left side—probably the same one I left through this A.M. and one very high window on the right side, approximate twelve inches high and three feet wide. The only catch was that it was nearly ten feet from the ground. We looked around futilely for a makeshift ladder. He sensibly nixed my idea of piling one oil barrel on top of the other, replacing it with a suggestion to have me stand on his shoulders. Yes, his shoulders—those very, very ample and accommodating bodacious beams branching out from his thick neck—not gross like a football linebacker neck—to see what was going on behind Building Number One.

Keeping in mind that I was still decked out in my pink and black Chanel, I was somewhat wary about the exposed position I would soon be in, what with him being able to catch an eyeful of all my business once I was atop his massive tree trunk. I scolded myself for minding my mother all these years by always wearing clean and hole-free underwear just in case I was ever in an accident. Well, this was no accident but for other reasons I regretted not extending the loan from Marie-Louise's wardrobe to include a wispy pair of black silk briefs instead of the white 100% cotton Hanes for Her high-tops I was so comfortably wearing today.

Oh well, too late. I hiked up my skirt, took both of his sinewy yet tender hands, put my right foot on his left knee and up, up and away I went—one hundred and forty-three point five pounds of me seemingly with the strength it takes to lift a sack of flour. I had to mentally slap myself in the face to snap out of this state of ga ga, but there was something so powerful and mesmerizing about this humble gentle giant, I found it extremely difficult to concentrate on the serious reality that I could very likely be on the verge of solving my very first crime—something big. Something of very possibly international proportions.

How's the view up there?, he whispered.

I wanted to say *how's the view down there?,* but of course just couldn't. I just said, *nothin' in this one,* and he whisked me back down to the ground with the grace of a gazelle.

Be still my beating heart….

Building Numbers 2, 3, and 4 were all empty. By the time we hit Building Number 5, we had our routine down pat. I imagined we were the famous Zbora Family Hungarian Acrobatic Act rehearsing for their sold out performance tonight at Barnum & Bailey's Circus: Powdered hands, firm clasp, foot-on-knee, hup and up.

I rubbed the caked on dirt away from the glass on the last window and found what we were looking for except for one thing—the players involved had split. The room was empty of people but the hospital set-up was still pretty much in tact. I gulped and jumped down.

Be still my beating heart….

Oh, my God, Philippe, we should have followed the black limo. It looks like we missed them by seconds! Why did you listen to me, I'm just a dumb P.I. who never ever got it right so why should today be any different?

I didn't really get into the self-evaluation of my inept investigative talents, I merely offered the opinion about the black limo being our figurative bad guy.

Hey, let's don't waste any time dwelling on wrong decisions, he said logically. *Let's just concentrate now on picking the place apart to find a new lead.*

Now why can't I think like you?—you hunka' hunka' burnin' love, I thought. I'm such an erratic plan maker during moments of stress.

We went around to the side door. Philippe positioned his .38 just in case we hit a surprise. I held on to the twisted belt of his raincoat—my lifeline, as it were, and we tiptoed inside.

The room reeked of alcohol, both the medicinal and recreational kind, bottles turned over with contents not yet completely drained, and about a half dozen cans of infant formula still in a grocery bag. The sheets on the well-worn birthing bed were more red than white. I didn't want to think of the fear and agony the three young girls—and probably countless others—had gone through in recent days.

Philippe took one end and I took the other. I really and truly forced myself to concentrate now so my infatuation with the inspector took an immediate back burner position the moment we entered the room.

I sorted through mounds of dirty linen, discarded syringes, cotton balls, empty drug bottles: Percanol, Penicillin, Demoral, Valium, Phenobarbital, and Pitocin for inducing labor. It was enough to put half the residents of Paris in the ozone. A mortar and pestle containing the crushed remains of one of the above mentioned pharmaceutical products made me shiver and I knew why. The quote unquote "sleeping" newborn infants had obviously been drugged to keep them out of the way until they were lovingly handed over to their unsuspecting new parents. How did that stupid waste of human skin "doctor" know how much was enough, not enough, or too much to administer to a five pound, eight hour old little creature? Trial and error?

Darra, I think I found something. Come here, my true love whispered from across the room.

Anything you say, Lover. Okay, I regressed a bit, I admit.

Whatcha' got? I really said.

Take a look at this.

He was kneeling in the far corner where the baby nursery was still located but was empty except for one bassinet. In his palm was a small piece of bronze metal. It had a red and black striped ribbon looped through it. There was a cross on one side, a Latin insigna: *Patria non immemor* on the other. I took it from him. Clueless, I handed it back and said,

Yeah, and?

Well, I guess I shouldn't expect you to know what it is as you are not French, but I will tell you that it is a very special medal, "La Médaille de la Résistance" worn only and always by freedom fighters with the Résistance Française in World War II.

Yeah, and?

I know for a fact that Antoine Trudeau was a member of the French Resistance.

I didn't know if we were on the same wave length or not. Up until now we had been. From the moment we met at Café de l'Afrique, we seemed to have matched-up like two peas in a pod, peanut butter and jelly, rum and coke, potato chips and onion dip, nachos and margaritas, et cetera. Just a perfect combination, we were.

Wait a minute, I said. *Are you implying that Trudeau could be involved with Mabouk in a totally other function—other than what we've been told by his wife? I mean, you don't think...*

My hand unconsciously rested on the tiny mattress in the empty bassinet. I cringed. It was still warm. I could almost smell the fresh newness of Baby X, now in transit. I even imagined I could hear a faint wimpering cry in the distance. I *shhhed* Philippe with a finger and strained my ear in the direction of the room where I had been held captive.

Ahhhhhhh.

It was just a pitiful little sound but it was not my imagination. I knew that for doggone sure.

Twelve

We ran toward the room bumping into each other when we reached the door opening, just like a couple of circus clowns.

The room was much like I remembered. There wasn't a window in this room so it felt like it was always ten o'clock at night. The natural light from the larger room beamed in, giving us something to work with. The stench was hard to describe: a combination of old cheese, human waste, and that rotten egg smell of a dead mouse or rat. I crazily thought of Pete and Stephanie, hoping I wasn't smelling either one of them and quietly wished them well.

Ahhhhhhhhhhhhhaaaggggghh, we heard ever so faintly from the left corner.

I clutched Philippe's enormous hand as we cautiously moved toward our next surprise.

Little Girl Beige was lying in a pool of blood, her vacant eyes seeming to cast a gloomy illumination to the dimness we had to work with. She had an ineffective old sheet between her legs to sop up the blood. She was paler than before but not quite as drained as the other lifeless bodies piled three high in the darkest corner of the room. I recognized the girl on top as the one I witnessed in active labor just a few hours ago. The other two must have given birth earlier and were discarded before I arrived on the scene. I didn't see the redhead.

I was too sickened to exclaim anything. I broke the iron grasp I had with Philippe's hand and dropped to the floor to take the scared child in my arms. I gently scooped her up and moved her away from the decomposing child mothers as if doing so would somehow protect her from her inevitable fate—a disposable baby machine. She was still alive, but barely. Her limp body molded to mine like a bean bag. Cradling her to my pounding chest I caressed her face and matted hair with my free hand and after a few moments lifted her head to look into my eyes.

She tried to speak. *Mmmaaaa. Mmmaaaa. Maaaa. Maaaa. Saaaay.*

Ma ma say.

Was she crying out for her mother? What?

Mmmmaaa Mmmmaaaa Saaay, she moaned almost inaudibly.

With my face just inches away from hers, I pulled out a reassuring expression from my endless expression supply, kissed the top of her forehead and lied:

It's okay. It's okay. Everything will be all right, sweetie. Mama is here. You'll be fine, I promise. We're going to take very good care of you and your precious baby. It's a little girl, you know. She looks just like her mama—beautiful. You'll be very proud of her. Don't worry, okay, sweetheart? Mama is here. Everything is going to be all better. We're going home now. We're going home.

She missed my last sentence. With eyes still wide open, she had gone Home. I closed her eyes with two fingers, accepted Philippe's clean white handkerchief to respectfully cover her face and mouthed a short prayer with a painful lump the size of a baseball in my throat.

I couldn't cry. I was past crying. I gently placed her head down on the wooden floor and slowly got up. When I got up, I collapsed along side of her. Philippe, understanding soul that he is, picked me up and bodily carried me to the door. On our way out, I heard a familiar scratching sound which led me to witness the inexhaustible Pete and Stephanie going to town once again, this time with an audience of a few of their offspring.

Life goes on.

We were back in the car in minutes and Philippe immediately radioed in for assistance. The squad car arrived simultaneously with the ambulance. I stayed in the car while he took them back to instruct them on how to handle the collection of evidence from the warehouse and to arrange for the coroner to take the dead mothers away. With a few minutes to myself, I reclined in the passenger's seat, closed my eyes and made an attempt to doze off. *Ma ma say. Ma say.* Something about the way she said it made me repeat it over and over in my mind. I couldn't get it out my head, just like a moronic, yet effective T.V. jingle.

I went back to yesterday, my meeting with Jacques, my imprisonment, my escape, my meeting with Marie-Louise today and the reprehensible tale of how they—she and Antoine—had become involved with Mabouk in order to fulfill a simple wish to become parents. I racked my brain to try to remember every detail of her story: Marie-Louise is hospitalized for depression...Malika, the trustworthy, motherly nurse's aide compassionately offers help...Antoine goes to Marseilles on business...Brings home new baby instead...Antoine called away again to Marseilles on Angelique's birthday...Upon his return, Antoine breaks down and confesses shameful details to Marie-Louise...Another urgent meeting in Marseilles...Poof...Antoine disappears.

Mar-seilles. Ma ma say. MA SAY. Could it be? Was the dying girl giving us a critical clue? *Marseilles?* Was Mabouk and his people on their way Marseilles?

My heart replaced the baseball in my throat and I leaped out of the police car to catch up with Phillipe, who was heading back to meet me.

Philippe! I know where they went. They are on their way to Marseilles in that black limo. I just know it.

What? Whadaya' mean, Marseilles? That's at least a five hour drive from here and besides what makes you think they're going there anyway?

I don't know why yet. I just know it, that's all. The girl. She was trying to tell us something. She wasn't calling out for her mother at all. She was trying to say MAR-SEILLES. Don't you get it?

He got it. Or at least he pretended to get it since we had no other solid leads to follow.

Okay, Darra. I'm gonna go with this one. Get in the car and I'll radio in to headquarters on the way. I'm sure we'll be able to take a Gendarmerie Nationale helicopter to get us there faster.

He did just that as well as advising the auto route highway patrol service, the C.R.S., to be on the look-out for a black limousine pulling a trailer heading south on the E-15. License number unknown. He instructed them not to apprehend but to follow and report their location to us in the air.

It took us fifteen minutes to reach the waiting helicopter on top of the Air France office building in the 17th Arrondissement, the closest landing pad to our entrance back into the city. We left his police car double parked in front of the building, took the elevator to the 22nd floor and ran to the gigantic buzzing Dragon Fly waiting to deliver us to we didn't even know where yet.

Philippe yelled out something to me as we climbed aboard but the whir of the spinning blade was so deafening, I couldn't make it out. So knowing I was safe, I turned my head away from him so he couldn't read my lips and screamed at the top of my lungs:

I love you tooooooooo!

Will I *ever* grow up?

We had about an hour en flight to work on our next plan but in the meantime Philippe told the pilot to stay close to the Auto Route du Soleil in case we got lucky and spotted Mabouk's car on the way.

Darra, are you sure you've told me everything you can remember? We've gotta' have something more concrete to go on. Where in the hell do we start in a city the size of Marseilles?

Oh, buggeration. Now the pressure was on me. I hate it when the pressure is on me.

Okay, okay, let me think a minute. Give me a few minutes, okay?

All right, but try to recall every conversation you had with these guys as well as Madame Trudeau since yesterday.

With that he unstrapped his harness, climbed up front to sit next to the pilot, all the while teasing me with a full on view of his Herculean buns on his way over.

I closed my eyes and started with practically the moment I arrived in Paris...

But I was too tired. No sleep going on two days. Before I knew it I caught myself taking a couple of long deep breaths, relaxing my aching body to about the consistency of an overripe banana and escaping to my quiet place...

It is summer. I am gliding through the French countryside in a brightly colored hot air balloon. The balloon just barely skims the tops of the clumps of trees and lavender colored hills beneath us. We are so close to the ground that I can smell the fragrance of rosemary, thyme and sage growing wild on the hills of Provence. It is so silent I can hear the gnats and the odd humming dragon fly splat against the huge passenger basket I am riding in. My windswept silky blond hair flows in the right direction at all times, a fresh, clean and glowing look of love paints my wrinkle free face. A complete khaki African safari outfit, except for the pith helmet and jungle boots, covers my still slender frame. I am barefoot. The compartment is quite roomy—large enough for me and for my fellow passenger, a blond maned seraph who falls from the sky into my basket just as we are coasting over the Châteauneuf-du-Pape region. My celestial fellow passenger starts massaging my feet. His authoritative palms knead the soles of my feet while he sings *"I'd like tah get you, on a slow boat tah China...."* He tells me how beautiful I am, but more importantly, how he finds my passion for righting wrongs at any cost and coming up with solutions to complicated problems, a real turn on. He's right and I know it. I never felt so brilliant...or beautiful. I excuse my petite left foot enveloped in his massive hands to get up to turn on the helium full blast to zoom us over to the coast, all the while enjoying an absolutely perfect glass of the above mentioned regional wine, red and robust, with half a loaf of hearty French country bread smeared with a creamy cheese delicately flavored with garlic aux fines herbes—also from the region. As we approach a busy seaport, my discerning eye picks up a huge white ship heading slowly out to sea...probably in the direction of China. I expertly turn down the helium valve on the basket, proficiently perform all the moves necessary to land this baby on a dime and walk hand in hand with my fellow passenger toward the horizon, the sun setting on the glistening sea.

I started to take my three deep breaths to finish my routine and convince myself how unconditionally I do love me, but before I could finish I was shaken out of my Alpha level of consciousness by a very familiar looking big, yet adorable hand.

Darra, wake up. We'll be in Marseilles in twenty minutes. Did you come up with anything else?

*Um, well, ah, as a matter of fact...*I stalled around a little. I only needed those few seconds to realize I did come up with something else.

Yeah, Philippe. I did. Listen, I know Marseilles is a big city; has a huge North African population and lots of illicit things go on there, but Mabouk has a special reason to go there—not just to get lost among other deviants like him.

What are you getting at?

Okay, here's the deal. Marseilles is the largest port on the Mediterranean, right? Mabouk's got cargo he's got to get out of the country and what easier way to avoid extensive customs questions than by sending it sea cargo? Whadayathink? Am I going someplace with this?

His eyes lit up and he gave me an ear to ear smile. His lips came dangerously close to brushing ever so lightly passed my cheek as he scrunched over to direct the pilot to find a pad nearest Gare Maritime de la Joilette. There we would find the Port Information Office and hopefully more fuel to find Mabouk before his ship sailed.

We touched down at the edge of the *Jardin du Pharo,* a large grassy park in the center of town at the mouth of the Vieux Port. We climbed down from the helicopter and signalled the pilot to leave us to wait for the Marseilles police, scheduled to meet us at any minute. I shooed away a scrawny, gray striped cat from a park bench and waved over to Philippe.

The park was quiet—a playground in one corner with an empty merry-go-round waiting for passengers other than the two cats huddled together and dozing on the seat of one of the carousel cars. More cats dominated the park benches and shady areas under the shrubs. A tipped over plastic container with what was left of three or four fish heads was being pawed into by a gang of hungry tomcats fighting over the last dusty eyeball. But the real focal point of the park is a palace built by Napoleon III for his one time Lady Love, Empress Eugénie, or so I was told. The police van arrived just as I was about to visit one of my quiet places again. My prince and I left the castle grounds via a waiting Marseilles police van. Not exactly a horse drawn golden coach, but I'm a real good fantasizer.

Thirteen

Port of Marseilles, Saturday evening

The Marseilles police had been radioed before we landed so they immediately whisked us off to the Port Information Office at the miles long harbor and dockyards. The Marseillesais Harbor Master's assistant was just finishing a hearty bowl of bouillabaisse when we walked in through the glass door. He was killing two birds with one stone by wiping his bowl clean with his forefinger—he must've been out of bread—then he tossed the "clean" bowl on top of a short file cabinet next to his cluttered desk. He wiped his mouth off with the versatile sleeve/napkin of his regulation Port Authority blue cotton shirt, then gave us a bawdy expression that excreted vulgarities even before he opened his mouth. I chuckled to myself. He didn't scare me. Are you kidding? With my own personal Guardian Angel standing so close I could smell his clean warm breath heating up the back of my neck? No. In fact, I could hardly wait for this employee who didn't like his job to open his mouth, until he did. His fish breath almost knocked me over. I stood back and let Philippe do the talking.

Bonsoir Monsieur, mon nom is Philippe Clement de la Police de Paris et e'est Darra van Zandt. Nous voudrions voir le liste des ports avec tous les bàteaux arrivés le dernier semaine et les horaires de départ aujourd'hui ou les prochains jours....cargaison et passager, s'il vous plaît.

He politely asked for the haven list of all ships, cargo and passenger, arriving in the last week including today, and their departure schedule.

Apparently we were unaware of Poisson Breath's dinner hour. He spurted a few obscenities under his foul breath while licking his burley fingers, then wiped them across the last clean sleeve before tugging at the file drawer in front of him. Within five minutes he provided the info, however impolitely I must say. He chucked it across the counter and walked away and back to his din-din without even a *s'il vous plaît* or an apology to us for his poor attitude. Oh well. We had what we were after anyway. Registered ships scheduled to arrive or depart, including embarkation points as well as destination points from Marseilles with their ETA's and ETD's.

The Pearl of the East: Cargo ship. In port since yesterday from Bangkok. Departing tomorrow for New York.

Antonio de Martalona: Cargo ship. Expected tomorrow from Caracas. Docking for one week for repairs. Destination Antwerp.

S.S. Golden Empress. Passenger ship out of Athens. In port. Departing at 11:00 o'clock tonight. Destination Palma, Majorca.

Marie du Mer: Cargo ship. In port. Departing in three days for Sydney.

The Ibn Nasser Toula: Cargo ship. Arrived this morning from Oran, Algeria-Departing at midnight for Southampton, England.

Hmmmm. Stop.

We stopped right there. The *Ibn Nasser Toula* just in from Algeria was sailing at midnight. It was eight thirty now. Philippe contacted the captain of the harbor precinct to request back-up assistance at the waterfront commencing at 11:00 P.M. Philippe gave him all the details and the Marseillais police captain assured him that he would be prepared with the S.R.P.J. de Marseilles, their French SWAT team, to go in when necessary.

Capt. Gaudette was kind enough to leave a police van with us so we took a half hour to grab a bucket of kebabs, a take-away container of tabouli and two bottles of water at *Chez Ahmad's Snak Shak*, and drove up to *Notre-Dame-de-la-Garde*, to scarf down, regroup our thoughts and cogitate over our Plan. The hilltop nineteenth century basilica is crowned with a gilded Virgin, "Our Guardian Lady" in English, sort of a French Statue of Liberty, who seems to be smiling down and embracing the melting pot of Marseilles. The view was magnificent but from up here one couldn't really see or smell the reality of down below. That's probably why she's smiling. If she only knew.

By the time we reached back near the harbor, I told Philippe that nature was calling but I really wanted to assess my make-up situation, my outfit and in general see if I was still knock-out cute. I know I have a runaway imagination but I could swear that at least twice during our quick hillside *al fresco* dinner Philippe dug into the shish kebabs at the precise same moment I did forcing us to make sensual greasy finger contact. Is it just me or does that sound a lit-tel bit like a flirtatious gesture?

I ducked quickly into the ladies room at a service station and scraped away the three years of pollution from the mirror over the sink. Sometimes I wonder why I bother. Here I am, using *the* most expensive bathing beads and shampoo, *the* most expensive make-up and was wearing a killer designer outfit—a combination that should allow a gal at least twelve hours of guaranteed sophistication and beauty, right? Not. My hair was starting to frizz-rin up, probably because we're near the sea, and my make-up was almost totally gone from my face. Fortunately, I had inadvertently gone off with Marie-Louise's Germaine Monteil collection in my borrowed black leather and obligatory gold chains hand bag, so I was able to make all the touch-ups necessary to bring me back to where I was, honey....Knock. Out. Cute. And I was beginning to like my hair a bit wild. Yeah, a bit reckless. A bit tigress-ish. My leopard print T-shirt would go good right now.

Grrrrahhhh.

I dabbed out a couple of kebab sauce stains on my skirt and smashed a tiny bit of chewing gum on a very, very skinny run in one of my silk stockings, but for the most part, I looked great.

Knock. Out. Cute.

Philippe was waiting with the motor running.

It was 9:00 o'clock. We had arranged to meet Capt. Gaudette at the rear entrance to the Harbor Master's office at 11:00 so that meant we had two hours to work on our strategy for when Mabouk and his entourage arrived with their cargo to board the Nasser Toula.

The docks were bustling at this time of night and since this was my first time at a port this size I had no idea if it was normal or not. It gave us sufficient cover, though, to stroll along the basin and pinpoint the location of the ship's berth. We passed six honkin' big freighters, a five hundred passenger cruise liner, the Singaporean Queen, and the smaller, ritzy titzy 75 passenger liner, The S.S. Golden Empress, which was dwarfed in between the Queen and the Morikone Maru, a rusty wad of steel three times the size of my house.

My house. Yikes.

My guilty heart flipped. I hadn't checked in with Marielle and Christina since last night. But they aren't even expecting me until late tomorrow afternoon, so unless I end up in Algeria or England, or the hospital—or even worse—I should be home in time to tuck Christina in tomorrow night. We can have a quickie wedding for Barbie & Ken while she brushes her teeth or something.

After we walked about a mile along the waterfront and noted the berth name assigned to the Nasser Toula, we turned around and headed back to the van to wait for Monsieur Mabouk. Most of the ships appeared to be full of life inside, crew members either sprucing up for going ashore for the night or the unlucky ones setting up card games to pass the long night as they pulled ship's duty.

The Golden Empress was dimly lit, twinkling white lights barely advertising her subtle presence. Sort of an elegant little firefly waiting to flitter away. I imagined myself flittering away with a partner of my choice to some safe haven.

As we approached the other side of the Empress, I turned back to take a last glance at her for what I thought would be just a look of envy, but lo and behold,

Surprise. Surprise.

Fourteen

Unless they all look alike, I could swear that I was watching the drooling Arabic woman I saw sleeping back at the warehouse boarding the Empress with a curly headed kid on her back.

I quickly pulled Phillipe behind a container destined for Hong Kong, and pointed to the clean, white ship directly in front of us.

The woman was followed by the red headed teenager, no longer with child, moving very slowly. Behind the girl, Jacques and Henri, both dressed in ship's whites, carried a three foot long and two foot deep rattan basket. Bringing up the rear, Rahib Tahar, the doctor, staggered up the gangplank lugging a huge black trunk with rubber wheels.

We waited five minutes until it appeared that Mabouk was either not with them or that we missed him getting aboard, but when I knew it was safe, I turned to Philippe and proceeded to identify all the passengers, in order of good guy/bad guy in case it came down to fire power at some point.

It was only 9:15 and Captain Gaudette wouldn't be here for another hour and forty-five minutes. Philippe's mobile couldn't seem to get a signal at the harbor so we had to find another phone to update the captain on new time, different ship. We stood up from behind the container to do just that but eagle eye Hank had just gone on first shift guard duty leaving us unable to move left or right without him spotting us. The dock was fairly well lit up and I knew he would i.d. me immediately.

Here's where Hank's weakness for anyone cuter than him gave us a fortunate advantage: A young Algerian girl—a beautiful, young, hard working Algerian girl, dressed in a deliberately skin tight purple mini-dress and gold and purple platform spike heels, strutted down the dock obviously on a mission. Hank took one look, flipped the glowing butt of his cigarette overboard and caught her attention just as she was about to miss out on her highest rolling customer of the evening. With some embarassing hand language, giving away one or two of the offered services, they negotiated over the basic price and what looked like a Round-The-World special. We hoped he'd go for the Round-The-World deal which would afford us more time. Once the messy matter of money was finally settled, Hank and his companion disappeared and we slipped away from behind the container and onto the ship's deck.

We started with the first lighted porthole, which was the ship's nursery—five bundles in five beds, the rattan basket opened and empty in the middle of the floor. Tahar was organizing his traveling pharmacy, mashing up tablets with a spoon in a shallow glass.

Nighty night, sweet babies, I whispered softly as wild rage rushed through every cell of my body.

The next cabin jailed the red-haired girl. She was lying on the bed, her knees drawn up to her chest. She rocked back and forth on the mattress. Post partum cramping, I diagnosed. She was twisting one clump of her curly hair so tight that it was in real danger of breaking right off at her scalp. Her face was dirty and tear stained, and like all her little friends before her, she looked terrified as hell.

We quietly moved down to the next porthole. Now this scene I could enjoy. We must have missed Mabouk's boarding because there he was, all 5'4" of him—a runt of a runt really, muscling around the 6'1" Jacques until Jacques fell to the floor, put one hand up over his precious face and the other hand down to protect his precious parts, and waited for the next blow. He got it in both of the anticipated sensitive areas. Then the wuss doubled over, spitted out a front tooth and in an extremely ungentlemanly manner, grabbed his groin.

Bad Karma, I'd say.

The last lighted porthole had the navy blue curtains partially drawn. In the only visible corner of the cabin, the Arabic woman was involved in some heavy conversation with someone on the other side, and the little Terrible Two blond toddler dressed in a white sailor dress roamed around the cabin pulling down anything and everything within arm's reach.

Darra, I hafta call Capt. Gaudette. We can't expect to take on this gang by ourselves. I've gotta get to a phone and get him here now.

I knew he was right. He always is. But I had this personal vendetta thing going and I didn't want to be deprived of any vengeful gratification I had been counting on up until now.

You stay here. Out of sight. And I mean it, Darra. Just stay put here under this tarp, he whispered as he positioned me in between two lifeboats.

Oh, delicious. He must really care, I thought.

Okay. Okay, I said reluctantly. *But geez, Philippe, hurry back in case they decide to set sail early. And don't let Gaudette come in too fast. We can't afford any mistakes. I just gotta' get those kids outta' there, ya know what I mean? I mean, ya know what I mean, Philippe? Do ya?* I was all hyped up and scared and tired and would have wished that this whole adventure was a dream if it wasn't so damn exciting.

If I'm not back in ten minutes—it's nine thirty-five exactly—check your watch—if I'm not back in ten minutes, go over the side here, swim over to the dock and call Gaudette at the precinct. Do you hear me? Here's the number.

Yeah, right. Like I'm really going to jump into the drink with this pink suit on.

Sure, okay. Got it. Lay low. Ten minutes max. Jump overboard. Swim to dock. Call Gaudette. Got it. Now get going.

We pressed up against each other in the narrow space between the two boats as he passed me to get to the other side. For a split moment I was sure I felt his manhood but it turned out to be his other gun, the one he just pulled out and cocked as he slipped away into the night.

Oh, Darra, Darra, Darra. You are simply *toooo* much, girl.

As soon as Philippe was out of sight I tiptoed back over to the most interesting window of all—the half closed one with the Arabic woman, who I finally decided was Malika, the goody-good nursemaid. She was going at it with her hands and oversized mouth but try as I may I couldn't see anyone else in the room. I did see another porthole looking into the same room on the other side, just around the corner from here—several yards away from where Philippe instructed me not to move from.

I took short, mindful steps and made a slinky right turn winding around the corner bringing me a mere six steps away from the other porthole. The first five steps worked out well but on the sixth I felt a sharp jab in my lower back and I had to conclude that it wasn't one of Philippe's "guns".

Funny how people's body odor can identify them without actually having to see them. I could have won a bet on recognizing Hank the instant the gun rammed into my tailbone reducing me into total submission. He yanked a clump of my hair, pulled me down so I had to half walk, half crawl as he led me into the ship's cabin corridor, past three doors and finally dumping me through the fourth.

Malika practically caught me as I came flying in but I found out soon enough that it was a freaky accident—she just happened to be there with arms outstretched trying to get a point across to a bound body wrapped like a mummy in a blue corduroy Lay-Z-Boy recliner facing the cabin wall. Malika released me as quickly as she had caught me and gave me a little kick in the ribs to cancel out my initial impression and make sure I knew she was one tuff dude-ette. She didn't have to convince me further. I knew I was once again in deep ca ca and if she knew me just a little better she'd know she wouldn't have to worry about any heroics coming from this littl'chick…I'll take her jive.

So. So you think you are a very, very clever Amereekan po-lice wohman, non? You think you can save this world, non? You think you are one smart, Amereekan copper, non? Why do you this, you foolish, foolish wohman? This eez not your business. This eez not your business, Missus lay-dee. You 'ave made a very wrong mistake, Mesuss Amereekan police detektif wohman.

She ranted on for five more minutes while she tied me up. The whole time her mouth was moving a golden front tooth reflected the track lighting on the ceiling giving off an eerie halo around her head. She was ugly. At least her attitude was ugly. I could hardly imagine how Marie-Louise and Antoine Trudeau could have been bowled over by her. She must put on a really good act to have gained enough confidence from them to allow her to care for their Angelique.

After I was securely, and I might add, claustrophobically bound, she went over to the Lay-Z-Boy, had a few more heated words with my cell mate and left the room.

The little toddler stayed.

The little toddler toddled over to me and sat down right next to my head. She leaned down and covered my face with runny nosed kisses, patted my head and said *"Aiiaaaiiiiiaaai,"* like I was the family pet.

Hello, little girl. Aren't you the prettiest little thing. What's your name? I guess I was just trying to pass time until Philippe and the troops arrived or maybe I was just keeping cool for the sake of the kid. Bravely acting as if my being tied up was nothing out of the ordinary could prevent the little mite from being more traumatized than she probably already was.

She started the face kissing again. She kissed away the tears beginning to seep down the side of my face. I looked up to the ceiling and whispered sincerely,

Hey, Sir, what gives? Can I have a Sign? Can I have a hint of a happy ending here? I'm waiting, Sir. Please tell me what to do next. In fact, could You get it started right away? It's just that having my hands and legs tied is about my least favorite position to be in, You understand? Thank You. I Love You. I'm waiting. How about that Sign?

Chéri, viens ici, came the voice from the Lay-Z-Boy.

Little "Chéri" answered the call. She ran over and looked up at the mummy in the chair. He spoke softly to her in French. I don't speak French but it sounded gentle and loving.

I don't know why neither one of us were gagged. Maybe because the ship's engines were loud enough to drown us out. Maybe the jerks forgot. Anyway, I managed to turn over on my stomach, do a caterpillar crawl over to the back of the chair and with a heave-ho, flipped myself back over on my back so I could formally introduce myself to the resurrected Antoine Trudeau.

Hello, I said very calmly. *My name is Darra. And you are?*

Trudeau, he said with resign, closing his eyes.

Antoine Trudeau, right?

Mais, oui, but how do you know ziz? He opened his eyes and took a good look at my face.

Non. What iz ziz? Who are you? You are not my wife. You are not Marie-Louizahh I know ziz, but you are looking like her. Why iz ziz,

119

you zay your name iz Dah-rah? You are wearing her clothez. What iz it now?

The only unwrapped portion of Antoine Trudeau's body was his head. He had a distinguished, refined face with soft, gray, wavy hair and sad gray eyes. He was not supposed to be in this humiliating predicament. He should be dressed in a Pierre Cardin suit, sitting behind a carved rosewood desk on a custom made soft leather executive chair instead of how he appeared before me—swathed in dirty white hospital bandages bound to a T.V. recliner.

Antoine, lookit. Just know that Marie-Louise is fine. She is very worried about you and Angelique and wants you both home. I didn't plan any of this, believe me, but it doesn't matter. We'll all be safe soon. The police are on their way. They'll be here any second now, I promise.

I just love the way I have the knack to reassure frightened people even when I, myself, am scared shitless.

Until then, however, how about telling me a little bit about what you, Monsieur, are doing here and how long have you been in that chair?

Ze story iz very long and complicated. And I 'ave been in ziz chair for ze three weekz.

I always think of the practical side of things. Like, if he's been in that chair for three weeks, how does he—you know—relieve himself when it becomes necessary?

I know most of it, Antoine. Marie-Louise has already told me about your involvement with Mabouk in order to acquire your daughter two years ago.

Oh, Mon Dieu. Mon Dieu. I am zo azhamed for everyzhing. I want only for Angelique to be returned to her mothzer and for me, I want only to die ze criminal death for what I 'ave done for ze zake of ze happinezz of my family. I do not dezerve to live.

He also had tears streaming down his face and sure enough, the little blond angel climbed up on the recliner, put her chubby little arms around his neck and kissed, patted and *aiiaaaii'ed* her papa until he was able to kiss her back and tell her everything was all right.

Now, this is just about the most heart wrenching experience I've ever been in. Here we are, two grown-ups—two parents to boot, totally incapacitated, and being cared for emotionally by a two year old. I didn't want to imagine the scars she'll suffer later as a result of this crazy role reversal incident.

Papa, Papa, je 'aime, Papa, she said as she jumped down to the cluttered floor, where she discovered a cardboard box of toys and suddenly escaped into another world. There was a pink, blue and yellow wooden set of alphabet blocks which she built three high and became disinterested in once they tumbled down; a brown teddy—too brown and boring; and a bright green Dino doll, with a red and yellow polka dot tie around his thick neck, purple brogans on his feet. She loved Dino. So would my Christina. The brighter the colors, the better.

I'm sure ten minutes had passed so I was beginning to get nervous about my promise to Antoine about being rescued. Philippe would surely be here by now unless he had been intercepted en route.

I flipped back over to my stomach and almost gouged an eye out with a pair of scissors that Angelique had dumped off the desk along with a ruler, pencils, letter opener and the empty red leather desk organizer they had fallen out of. The scissors were leaning on the desk organizer, points up, just millimeters away from my face.

Oh boy. Now this will be a stretch, I know, but it's worth a shot.

Angelique, sweetheart. Angelique, come baby, come. Come to Darra.

Angelique turned, looked at me and then went back to playing.

Angelique, baby, come. Come. Want cookie?

She looked at me again with a quizzical look and it was only then that I realized that the kid didn't understand English.

Angelique, bébé, voulez vous un biscuit?

She dropped Dino and came right over to me, sat down next to my face and exclaimed,

Le bisquit! Le bisquit!

Uno momento, I said in Spanish. Don't ask me why. Then I turned to Antoine, who seemed to be gazing into space.

Antoine, how do you say "scissors" in French? Can you tell Angelique to bring me the scissors?

Chéri, donnez les ciseaux á Madame.

The child genius promptly picked up the scissors and dropped them perilously close to the tip of my nose. Then she picked them up again and with expert dexterity opened and closed them several times, clipping off a sizable chunk from my bangs, the most crucial hair spot on my head.

Agghhhh, I groaned. If she only knew what an important role my bangs play in covering my weak eyebrows. At least I knew the shears were extremely sharp and although I feared for the kid cutting off a finger or something, I continued,

Antoine, tell her to cut the rope here, wiggling my crossed hands behind my back.

Antoine just stared straight ahead. Geez, I've seen that look before—on his wife. What is it with these Trudeau people? When the going gets rough, fade out? What? Looks like this two year old here will be the only other trooper working on getting us off this boat that is just about to shove off.

Angelique, chéri, couper. Couper. I think that means "cut" but I hoped she knew I meant the rope and not my fingers. I balled up my fists in case she got understandably careless and jiggled them in front of her.

She ignored my wiggling fists, said, *cou-pay* and with more attention to detail continued to chop off another critical hair spot—one whole batch on the side of my head.

Eweeewww, I whined.

Angelique, bèbé, non, non. No do. No do that. Couper. Couper. I repeated and shook my fists even more definitively.

Cou-pay, cou-pay, she gurgled as she evened off the other side of my hairdo then went for my eyelashes.

That's it, I cried, scrinching my eyes tight to save what little lashes I had left for a "woman my age".

Just when I thought all hope was gone, the angel finally got the first message and snipped off the twisted pantyhose cutting into my wrists. I grabbed the deadly weapon away from Angelique, released my ankles, gave her a hug, and crawled over to her father to check out his status.

He was going to be useless as far as escaping was concerned. Of course I felt for the guy but my first priority was freeing the babies and the redhead. I took the scissors and carefully cut through some of the miles of tape binding him to the Lay-Z-Boy, but once his legs and arms were able to move about, I told him he would have to work on the rest himself. He murmured *d' accord, d' accord*, and I grabbed Angelique to leave through the cabin door, if indeed it had been conveniently left open for me.

It wasn't.

I turned back to consider any other possibilities in the cabin, zeroed in on one of the portholes and wildly imagined that I saw a picture of

Philippe framed within the oval hole in the cabin wall. The picture smiled. And what a smile. It *was* my Philippe, my hero, my savior.

What a guy! What a day!

I unlatched the window and immediately recognized the enchanting fragrance that is just so him and said, *Philippe, I was so worried about you. Did you reach Gaudette? Get us outta here. Are you okay? I've got the Trudeau baby and this is Antoine Trudeau but what's the deal with the police? Are they here? Or not? Or what?* I always ramble when I'm nervous or tired and I was both.

Yes. Okay. Yes, I'm fine. No, not yet. They're on their way. He efficiently answered all of my questions all at once and told me to send Angelique through the porthole and I did. She had no trouble getting through but of course there was no hope for me exiting the same way.

The handle of the cabin door creaked and opened before I had a chance to come up with a reasonable plan, so I did the next best thing which was the first thing that came to mind: attack! It was Malika! When she saw me standing there, she, too, was taken aback. I took advantage of her momentary surprise, picked up a heavy brass table ornament that looked like an African fertility symbol and bonked her over the head before she could react. She went down like an anchor.

Nighty night, bitch.

We'll be back for you soon, Antoine. Try to move around a bit to get the circulation back in your legs and we'll be back to get 'ya, okay? Oh, and see if you can manage to tie up Malika here—and gag her, okay?

D' accord, he mumbled again. *Okay.*

I pulled the folded printout of the ship's schedule from my jacket pocket and found the Golden Empress' E.T.D.: 11:00 PM. It was 10:00 PM on the dot. We had an hour before the Empress was scheduled to depart for Palma, Majorca.

I slowly opened the cabin door, took delicate steps down the corridor and stepped out onto the deck and fresh sea air. With his spare hand Philippe gently pulled me to him and we had a group hug—my Big Angel, The Little Angel and me.

I thought I told you to stay put, Missy? He began to scold me in just the cutest way you could ever imagine—commanding yet loving.

Do you realize how much you put everyone in jeopardy because of your asinine, inept way of thinking? What is the matter with you? I thought you cared about these kids? Hell, Darra, just where do you come off thinking you can save the world, huh? He ripped into me with a definite change of tune.

Sorry, I said sheepishly.

He was ticked off but I'm sure he was just relieved to find me safe and had to vent his frustration somehow.

Okay, inspector. You're right. I'll do what you say from now on, sir. Shall I take Angelique, sir?

He glared at me with disgust and handed Angelique over to me.

When it hit me that he was genuinely pissed off with me, I was destroyed. How he could say such cruel things to me, I just don't know. Who knows if I'll ever be able to overcome my pain and carry on, however ineptly. If he only knew that my already marginal confidence level had just plummeted to a depth so deep that only a major miracle could possibly mend my shattered self-esteem, he would have thought twice before lambasting me so vehemently.

Get a grip, Darra, I encouraged myself.

Your name is Darra,
You're number one,
Your rep-u-tay-shun has just begun....

Come on, girl, you can do it…

Snap out of it, Darra. Don't go girlie on me now, he spat out with even more venom than before. *Give the child back to me and help me undo this lifeboat.*

I guess you never know with some people. I really thought there was something good between us. Something heavenly. Special. But no, he's just like all the rest of them. I handed Angelique to him and as he maneuvered with one arm, I went through the motions, but my heart was no longer in it. I undid my side of the boat and gently lowered it down to deck level following Inspector Clement's instructions to a T, as ordered.

So, what's our next course of action Inspector? That is, if I may be so bold to ask? I had a royal chip on my pink shoulder.

Damn it, Darra. He came over to my side of the boat, took my upper arm in his right hand put his face one inch away from mine and went on, *Darra. I'm sorry if I hurt you. I'm sorry if I was rough on you. I care about you and what happens to you, don't you know that? And I care about saving these kids and putting away the repugnant low-life running the operation. We would never have gotten this far if it hadn't been for your intuition....yes, perhaps your woman's intuition, but perhaps it was even more the instinct of an excellent detective as well. I need you, Darra, don't flake out on me now.*

His breath on my face was warm and sweet and he smelled like baby powder. How can ya stay mad at a guy like that?

Flake out? Me? Are you nuts? I was only being pensive for a few minutes while I contemplated our next move. Whaddayasay? Let's go in, Philippe!, I proclaimed with renewed faith in myself and an even bigger crush than ever on ze babeliciouz Inspector Clement.

Even with the ship's generator roaring, it could not completely muffle the blood curdling scream coming from one of the cabins.

We looked at each other, two peas in a pod once again, and started all over with our porthole peeping, Angelique in tow.

126

Fifteen

No matter where we put Angelique, we knew she would be in danger anywhere on the boat. We ran down the outside deck to the last cabin, where Antoine was still busying himself with securing Malika, and reluctantly passed his daughter back to him through the porthole while we investigated the scream.

I was impressed with the creativity Antoine used to restrain Malika. With what little there was available for such a task, he utilized his three week old bandages for her limbs and stuffed the handy Dino doll in her large mouth with only his little purple boots sticking out helplessly. I promised myself to buy Angelique another Dino…when we get out of here.

Malika was not a happy camper. She glared at me through the porthole. The daggers in her eyes relayed a message that was probably…*So, you think you are going to get away with this, don't you Missus Pol-ice Lay-dee wohman? You are mistaken. You are dead wohman. You are dead meat. I will use you to make pol-ice de-tek-tif sheeesh kebab. Dis iz my solemn vow, missus.*

On the other hand, she may have been secretly admiring me for my brilliant escape and would like to shake my hand if she could.

No matter. Even tied up she still spooked the bejeezus out of me. I intentionally lost eye contact and turned to Antoine.

Good work, Antoine, I said. *Now throw that Snow White sleeping bag over Malevecent here and you and Angelique hide under the desk or try to fit under the bed or in the closet—just stay out of sight. We'll be right back.*

But what iz ziz again? He whined. *You zay...you promize zhat we are zafe. You zay zhat ze police are here for uz. What iz now ze problem? You made ze promize to me.*

So sue me, Monsieur. Sue me for Breech of Promise. Sue me for Loss of Joy. For Pain and Suffering. I'm from California. It's to be expected. Sue me for Mistrust. He didn't realize he was nagging me. And. I. Do. Not. Like. To. Be. Nagged.

There's no serious problem, Monsieur. The police are here. We'll be back in a jif. Just get out of sight for a few minutes.

With the now familiar "nobody home" face again, he took Angelique in his arms and as we left the window he was making a half-hearted move to disappear under the bed.

The cabin next to Trudeau's was empty. The redheaded girl's room was next but the curtain had been drawn and although we couldn't see anything we could hear smothered screams coming from inside. The baby nursery was quiet, dimly lit and since we couldn't see Tahar from our vantage point, we suspected that he had joined in next door.

Capt. Gaudette signaled from the dock that he and his men, some fifteen sharpshooters of his elite S.R.P.J Special Police unit, were taking position on and around the Golden Empress and that—har har—I should high tail it out of there. I pretended like I didn't understand him, of course, and entered the corridor behind Philippe. I couldn't help myself. It wasn't me doing this. I'm basically Darra the yellow-bellied-chicken-liver under normal life situations. But this was not normal life. At that very moment I was Darra DooRight.

The door to the nursery was ajar making it easy to ascertain that the doctor was out. The rattan basket had been moved to the end of the room and was set up as Tahar's seafaring bar—three short, fat Old Fashioned glasses, a bottle each of Jack Daniels, Dewars and Bombay Gin sat ready with pouring spouts installed for neat pourings during the upcoming bumpy voyage. I dumped everything into the waste can and dragged the basket over to the middle of the room.

The babies were sleeping, of course, making it rather easy to load them carefully in the empty hamper still padded with a blue thermal blanket. One babe sucking both fists like mad opened his eyes, looked at me as if to say, *Mama, is that you mama? I'm hungry, mama. Aren't you going to feed me, mama?*

Then he closed his eyes and went back to his tiny fists. I closed my eyes and clenched mine.

Philippe and I carried the basket out to the hall to try to get it on the deck but when the sounds from the redheaded girl's cabin got louder and the door opened, we quickly ducked into another door on the right. We found ourselves in the galley. Well-worn seasoned pots and pans were secured to their nautical hinges, and shelves of savory Arabic spices and exotic herbs were neatly arranged above the shiny, black stove. Fresh veggies, a sack of dried lentils, slabs of beef, lamb, fish and other stores were stacked up high on the stainless steel counter tops. No one was gonna go hungry on this voyage—except for me maybe. I couldn't remember the last morsel to pass my lips. I was feeling downright gaunt. I liked it.

The galley was at the end of the grand dining room. We placed the basket under the far end of the long mahogany dining table standing in the middle of the room and draped a white linen table cloth down to the floor to keep it hidden while we were gone.

In the hall, Jacques had his back to us and Mabouk was facing the inside of the girl's cabin. Even with only a side view I could see a lecherous look of kinky arousal coming from his face. He turned quickly and went down to his cabin, probably taking a hard-on with him. His wimpy toothless bodyguard tagged along behind.

With me snugly suctioned like a leech to Philippe's back, we slid closely along the paneled wall of the corridor until we reached the middle cabin. With a swift kick to the cabin door, Philippe flew in to the room, tackled the doctor before he could make a drunken return and gun butted him on the back of his head to put him out for a while.

The redheaded girl was lying on the bed. She was not dead. She had a story to tell but she'd never be able to tell it. Her tongue had been cut out and what was left was wrapped up with so much gauze it looked like a bloody snowball in her mouth. Both of her hands wore matching bloody gauze mittens. She was covered in blood and her face was bruised; eyes swollen shut.

But she wasn't dead.

I remembered what Marie-Louise had said to me about the fate of these girls. She said that the lucky ones were killed. Now I knew what she meant. All of a sudden I didn't feel so sorry for the beige girl and the others we found dead at the warehouse. At least their nightmare was over. I looked at the girl on the bed and wondered what in the hell we were going to do with her when we got her out of here.

Gaudette was in the corridor with two policemen. We directed them into the cabin while Philippe quietly explained the sitch in French. One agent gently carried out the girl, one roughly dragged away the doctor and Gaudette stayed with us. He made a final plea with me to get off the ship, but once I gave him one of my famous dark brown looks: deadpan face, crinkled forehead and those bug eyes I used on Marie-Louise, he gave up.

The lights in the cabin and indeed the entire ship started to flicker; the engines made a purring noise. If I had been nice and safe at home in a cozy Dutch bar this could have just been an innocent last call for alcohol.

But this was a last call of a different kind. We were setting out to sea.

The lights went out for about three minutes. Completely out. I heard a thud that I prayed was only Philippe or Capt. Gaudette stubbing a toe in the darkness and I blindly groped around for either one of them. I wasn't choosy. I didn't want to make a sound but I couldn't control releasing a huge sigh of relief when I got hold of a hard, muscly arm. I knew that arm anywhere. That's my guy, I gushed. He'll know what to do, my guy.

He took my hand and led me back out to the hall. The urge to be enveloped in the safety of his arms was overwhelming, so I didn't fight it anymore. I drew myself close to him but stopped mid-hug. And then I noticed that his breath was warm but not sweet anymore. And his baby freshness had finally worn off. The lights flickered again and during the split second of light I realized that I was in another big pickle. A jumbo dilly.

When the light returned I noticed my guy was gone, along with the police captain. I was now reunited with a recent acquaintance—none other than Monsieur LaPointe—no longer dressed in simple country French farm attire, but looking rather fetching in a gray pin-striped Yves St. Laurent. All 237 hairs on his head were still neatly in position.

He led me back inside the same cabin.

Good evening, Madame. His English was perfect. Why am I not surprised? *You remember me perhaps? We meet again, Madame, and not by chance, but because of your persistence, shall we say, in being involved in a complicated matter that has nothing at all to do with you.*

The ship was now about five minutes out of the harbor and my stomach was starting to pick up the rhythmic roll that is usually so darn easy to get wrapped up in if there's nothing else to hold your interest.

What are you going to do with me, Monsieur LaPointe? I tried to be poised.

Tsk. Tsk. No, no, no, Madame. My name is not LaPointe. And that is The Point, he punned unintentionally. *You know too much. You know by now that I am Mabouk.*

Oh cheese n' rice. He just revealed dangerous information that I did not particularly want to know, given the situation. No fair.

Oh no, no, no, I protested. *I don't know that, Monsieur La Pointe. Mabouk is in the next cabin with that Jacques guy. You are just the thoughtful gentlemen who took me back to Paris when I was stranded on the highway. And, oh, may I say now that I am soooo sorry that I mistakenly gave you the wrong directions to my hotel. It was not intentional, trust me on that. I mean, you were sooooo kind to pick me up when no one else would. Can we take a rain check? I'm staying at the...*

Tut. Tut. Tut. You are a babbling female, he interrupted. *Are you not the slightest bit curious about why, I, of all the cars passing you, would want to give you a lift?*

Um. Um. Well, it did cross my mind, but...

But. But nothing. Whether it is your desire or not, you have become involved in our operation and we will be acting accordingly. You are here and you are going with us and we will treat you as we would any other female guest on our ship.

Is that a good thing?, I wondered, flashing back to the speechless girl who just left the boat. I don't think so.

The cabin door opened and a frantic Arab, the bartender I took for Mabouk at the café, entered with hands rapidly flailing about to emphasize his story. Of course I didn't understand Arabic, but the emotion in his voice told me it was serious.

Mabouk pushed me down onto the bloody bed and warned me to stay put. I did. He locked the door behind him and started screeching out Arabic orders to everyone in the hall. I didn't have the slightest idea what he was so hyper about but I was hoping it was the discovery that the babies were gone.

I drifted off into prayer:

Oh, God, please let it be so. Let the babies be safe. Let them be off the ship. Let my own children be safe. Let them remember their mom as a good mom. A mom that loved them very, very much, okay? I suppose You're getting ready to take me now, right? Okay, God. I'm ready to go. Oh, wait. One more thing. Let my Soul Mate find another soul mate. Maybe not quite as soulful as me, but enough to make him relatively happy anyway. And, another thing. I don't want all of my loved ones gushing over me when I'm gone. Maybe they can recall some of the not-so-loving things I've done all my life. That shouldn't be too difficult, and it'll be easier for them that way. And if they insist on an open casket—which I am totally opposed to, by the way— please, please make sure that my best friend, Ruthie is in charge of cleaning up my chin hairs and filling in my eyebrows. She'll know what to do. It's her forté. My sister, Aloncia—she'll simply have to perform a hair styling miracle on this chopped up head of hair. My baby sister, Lulu can prepare my skin for the last time with her highly successful Lulu's Earthworks Aromatherapy line, And my eldest sister, Sozahn—she gets to do my make-up.

I guess that's it. Your will is my will, dear Father. If my time is up, it's up. But I gotta tell ya, there's still a lotta fight left in me, Lord. If you could just find it in Yourself to decide that I can still be useful to You, I promise, promise, promise to work on my attitude and to be a better mother, wife and friend for as long as You so mercifully see fit to keep me here with You. Hey!, I just came up with another idea about foiling this Mabouk but I'm gonna need Your help. Oh, how stupid of me. You know my plan. You put it there. Sorry. Anyhoo, can You spring me this one last time? Or are You mad at me? Are You disappointed with me for that harmless flirtation with Inspector Clement? You did send him, did You not? There's nothing to it, really.

From my side it's totally innocent. We just happened to click, Philippe and me. Is he all right? You didn't take him back yet, did You?
So, Lord, it's in Your hands. I'll just lie here until You reveal our next step, okay? Okay.

P.S. Oh, and hey, don't forget about my ten percent tithing vow. I'm really serious about that. A done deal. Ten percent off the top.

No, make that twenty.

I felt seasick and the green-gray face I saw in the brass framed mirror on the wall across from me confirmed it. "death warmed over with bad haircut" I believe would be an appropriate description of how I looked and felt.

I missed Philippe. I didn't know what to do without him. I was overly optimistic in my last prayer when I said I knew how to bring Mabouk down. In truth, I was hopelessly helpless without Philippe.

I closed my tired eyes and must have fallen asleep for a while. I was awakened by the aroma of some wonderful ethnic dishes, probably couscous and a whole lamb on a spit. My stomach growled so loud I would have been embarrassed if Philippe had been there to hear it.

Philippe. It always comes back to Philippe. Oh, man, I got it bad and that ain't good.

Oh, Phil-ippe, I said again but this time out loud.

Oui? C'est moi. It's me. Under here.

Where? Philippe? Where are you? Is that really you? What happened?

Shhhh. Can't explain now. Don't worry. Shhh. Someone's coming, came a voice from under the bed.

Hel-lo Missus lay-dee wohman pol-ice detektif. So. So, you are still with us, dat is clear. You like us so much to leave am I not correct?

Shall I make you more comfortable, Missus gurl lay-dee copper? You make Malika unhappy mad. Dis is not good for you to live long.

I know I'm one to talk, but this Amazon had about a 75 word max English vocabulary.

Ah, hi ya, Malika. How ya doin'? Nice earrings. Nice shiny tooth. No, I'm fine. Really, I'm just fine right here. Don't fret yourself about me. I'm real comfy.

She ignored me and proceeded to empty the contents of the huge pockets of her African print dress: a couple of rolls of gauze, a roll of adhesive tape and an ace bandage. She organized them carefully on the table, turned to me and with a glittery toothy grin, sang, *Be back soooon, Missus.*

My mind raced not so far forward toward the brink of insanity...*Good evening. My name iz Malika and I'll be your server tonight. I'd like to recommend our special this evening which iz Shish-Kebab Tongue and Fingers a la Amereekan Pol-ice Detektif Wohman...*

I woke up in a cold sweat. I looked under the bed to tell Philippe about my bad dream but he wasn't there. Never was. It was all a dream. I was still on my own and wanted to cry like a baby so I did. I sobbed for five minutes, moaned for another three, then shot up in the bed completely rejuvenated.

Thank you Lord. I'm baaaaack...

Sixteen

A few minutes passed before Malika entered the cabin, this time for real.

So. Missus lay-dee woh-man pol-ice detektif gurl, what are we going to do with you now? You are a very stoopid gurl for pol-ice lay-dee, do you know dat? Do you know dat I am unhappy for you hitting my head? Do you like I hit your head? Or something else, maybe? Come with me and do not say a word or I make sure you do not say word again. Do you understand my story, Missus?

Ah, sure do, Malika, I meekly responded as she dominantly guided me down the corridor to the galley and dining room.

The bony bartender was now pulling cook's duty. He tossed pounds of cut up lamb and vegetables into a massive iron pot and generously flowered the mixture with fresh herbs and spices from the orderly rack above the stove. You gotta hand it to this culture. They sure know and love their food. Nothing comes between it, looks like.

At the head of the long dining table sat the nervous Mabouk and his toothless and finally frumpy accomplice, Jacques. Malika put me at the far end of the table then lumbered back to sit on the right of Mabouk who was rapidly cracking and popping pistachio nuts into his mouth with obvious experience.

They were all looking at me. Even the cook. So I looked back at them. They stared back at me. I guess it was my move.

I started. *So, guys, where are we going? Can you at least tell me that? Mr. Mabouk, sir, I only bother to ask because, and you can verify this with Jacques, right, Jacques? I have a little girl back home in…well, never mind where…but she's waiting for me and if I can just give a quick call home to check on things…you know how it is…just a quick phone call, that'll be all I need and I won't trouble you guys again. Swear. I'll even give you my solemn word to help you out just as much as I possibly can. You know something else? Is my face red! I do believe I totally misjudged your philanthropic work. I know you must be a verrrry humane person to want to match up children with childless couples—the method with which you accomplish this is, of course, hard to understand, but, hey! Judge not…lest ye be judged, right?*

I could not believe that the bullshit I was hearing was coming out of my own mouth.

Awww shad-dup, woh-man. Malika lashed at me.

Okay, okay. And I shad-dup.

Mabouk pounded his Vienna sausage fist on the table and the room became still—only the sizzling of the braising lamb trickled through the silence.

It was obvious that everybody was in trouble. Not just me. His whole team was about to be castigated for screwing up probably way back from the get go.

"Number one", he pointed a stubby thumb up in the air, *Henri is gone,* he continued. *Tahar is gone. Henri was minding guard and missed the Marseillais police entering from the dock. The swine bastard SPRJ are extremely skilled in silent approach maneuvers and they overcame Henri in the black night. They were also somehow able to capture the doctor, take the the girl as well as Antoine Trudeau and his child when they left their cabin* <u>and</u>*...my imbecilic remaining colleagues, all five infants promised for tomorrow's delivery. This is most distressing. Except for the large police detective who I was able to get rid of myself, we have only this stupid blond woman to take care of.*

Get rid of? Get rid of? What did he mean, police detective he got rid of? When did I last see Philippe? Before the lights went out. We had just pulled out of the harbor. Oh, God.

For the first time in a long time I wasn't thinking first of my own skin. Sure, I knew I was the only blond woman in the room. Okay, the only stupid blond woman. I knew they weren't going to let me make that phone call or drop me off at the next port with airfare back to Amsterdam. I knew that. I'm not *that* stupid. But right now I was grieving for Philippe. My eyes were stinging with pain. My body went numb, arms falling to my side, legs flying out uncontrollably in front of me so much so that I almost slipped under the table. Even though my right foot was almost paralyzed, I could still feel it being obstructed by a large object.

Nobody was paying attention to me at the end of the table. They knew I wasn't going anywhere and Mabouk had what was left of his committee rapt in what he was saying...or rather screaming from his throne. I performed a primary survey, making sure cook was cooking, Mabouk was preaching, and puppets were listening before I chanced a subtle glance under the drooping white table cloth to see what my right foot was hitting.

It was the basketful of babies.

Seventeen

While the berating of the troops continued, I scanned the dining room for other exits. I swear, if I had to make one more escape attempt I might have to join a circus and make some money at it like Houdini did.

Hey, Father, did you hear that? Don't forget, a full twenty percent of that money is Yours if You could just start revealing the way outta here sometime soon.

Ga ga wah, I heard ever so weakly in the vicinity of my right foot. From the basket to be precise. Nobody else heard. They were all wrapped up with who was to blame for what and why.

Ga ga wah. Again. I coughed a sort of *ga ga wah* kind of cough. They all stopped and looked at me.

Ga ga wah. I coughed again with more drama added this time.

Dinnah iz now prepared, announced cook. Saved by the proverbial dinner bell.

The arguing stopped. Malika dragged the white tablecloth hanging over my end of the table to place the tableware, utensils and wine glasses upon. Atop a butane burner in the center of the table sat a gigantic black pot. Cook ladled out mounds of tasty looking food to the hungry perpetrators.

The table grew heavier with platters of shrimps, whole fish, salads of pickled tomatoes, chick peas, cucumbers and yogurt, a scrumptious looking pilaf and steaming loaves of oven fresh flatbread. Mabouk was engrossed with the challenge to scrape every conceivable edible morsel off a mutton leg. He used a ruby and pearl handled dagger to dig into the marrow of the clean bone then used it to pick the stringy bits out of his teeth for dessert.

Jacques was still nursing his new dental rearrangement so he was working on getting a spoonful of pilaf to enter the side of his mouth, an undertaking that was at best fifty per cent successful. The other fifty per cent made yellow saffronish stains on his white sailor suit. I would have found it more amusing if I wasn't in such a foul mood.

You'd think they hadn't eaten in days the way these guys fell into food unconsciousness. They were so out of the real world I think I could've just gotten up, said my good-byes—or not, and slipped out the door but I had to stay with the babies. I wasn't letting them out of my sight one more time.

The eaters were foolishly washing down every mouthful with a risky combo of cognac and champagne. I made a pleasant mental note that perhaps the repercussion to this daring concoction would be to my future advantage if I could bide my time a little longer.

Someone put on a cassette of an irritating Arabic Dean Martin full blast to which I added some finger snapping to help drown out the *ga ga wah's* now coming more regularly from the basket.

You hongry, gurl Missus?, Malika drooled out as she sucked on a bone. *Too bad, Lay-dee. Ummm. So deliziouz dat lamb is.*

She enjoyed teasing me. I was hungry enough to eat the wings off a low flying seagull but I wasn't about to give her the satisfaction.

No, no. I'm really stuffed, I fibbed.

The irksome music was so deafening I couldn't hear a word they said but they weren't talking all that much anymore anyway. The occasional robust belch was the only sound able to break the monotonous singsongy music.

Just when it looked like they were finished, more grub would arrive and they'd start all over again. This went on for what seemed like hours until some unexpected weather came out of nowhere moving the ship with an authoritative jolt, as if it had been ordered to get someone's attention.

Hmmmm. Thank You.

I grabbed each side of the table with my hands, clenched both ends of the basket between my wide spread legs and held on for dear life. My captors were not quite so well prepared and all four of them fell off their barrel chairs still with cutlery in hands, chow in mouths, booze in guts. They all pounced back, reaching out with greasy hands to secure the bubbling black cauldron in the center of the table before it rolled over like a bowling ball on the burnished parquet floor. But it was too late. The remaining contents erupted out of the pot like Mt. Edna before it bounced on the floor and started traveling at a good clip back towards the galley. The pot picked up velocity on its way so by the time it struck the stove, it forced another pot—a fry pot deep with oil, to turn over and feed the burners which had been left on to keep food warm.

The galley ignited first into an orange ball, then a black one, then I didn't know anymore. The oxygen in the room seemed to have been sucked out and replaced with granulated charcoal dust. Everyone was screaming—except me. Don't ask. I don't know why. With the basket still tight between my legs my only thought was to get it out of the inferno. I was at the far end of the room so my chances were slim to say the least, but that supermothersonic power overcame me and I carried on as if in a trance. I caught a liter bottle of sparking water rolling past me, whipped the stained white tablecloth off the cleared table, doused it and quickly wrapped it around my basket of babies the best I could.

The unrelenting sea seemed to want to swallow up the Golden Empress—and to be honest, I could understand why—but honey, wait til we get off, okay? I poured another half empty bottle of water over my head and body and tied a used napkin around my face for a mask and started to drag the basket to the door. Flames were licking my feet, burning them. The door, which appeared to be ten miles away, was taking on a reddish hue. I pushed on—babies now making uncomfortable noises inside—until I was just three feet away from the sizzling door.

The blast of the now flaming door leaving its hinges and hitting the deck rendered me temporarily deaf. It blocked out the helpless cries of Mabouk, Malika, Jacques and Cook. Silence. Just silence. And fire, of course.

And an open doorway.

My black flats felt as if they were melted to my feet and all the darn gold chains dangling from my pink Chanel singed my skin with the slightest contact. I was certain my lungs were barbecued. The only way I could continue was to hold my breath from this moment on— my focus being the open doorway and air. I was moving ahead, only inches at a time; the basket clutched in an iron grip that comes from that supermothersonic power thing.

I was outside. On deck. My hearing was coming back but I couldn't make out any more sounds from the dining room or galley. The whole rear of the ship was ablaze and I could feel a definite listing of the doomed vessel.

I remembered the lifeboat that I helped Philippe set down to deck level earlier so I dragged my precious cargo over to it. I removed the steaming tablecloth from around the basket and for the first time had a chance to open it to monitor the condition of the infants. There they were—all five—all awake and looking hungry, especially Hungry Jack at the end who was still trying to make a meal out of his fingers. No time to fall apart now. We were in a real sinking ship situation and I was not about to go down with it. I took five seconds to kiss their soft little foreheads in case I never got another chance and I closed the lid.

Lifting the basket on board was going to be another story. I turned a heavy deck lounge chair into a ramp. Clever. I then pulled the basket behind me as I walked backward up the chair ramp and on to the middle of the life boat. For precaution, I wove the straps of four life preservers through the handles of the basket, got out and tried to figure out how to use the pulley to lower the boat down to sea level. It was easy. Not only that. The ocean was calm again. Smooth as glass. I slid down the side of the boat on the pulley rope, joining the kiddies to release us forevermore from this hellish nightmare.

The rest should be easy. All I had left to do was feed the kids and take them home.

Home?

Eighteen

The Golden Empress went down moments after we pushed away from it. Not exactly in a blaze of glory, but more appropriately slipping like a flaming coffin full of demons down to its rightful grave. I could see only pitch darkness in every direction. Not even one single twinkling light to assure me that we were drifting toward some sort of civilization. Or something.

Nothing. Just dead quiet. And a smoldering black sky.

I checked the babies again and they appeared to be sleeping. I nervously felt their pulses and was relieved when they squirmed to my touch. They were still breathing for the moment, but without nourishment soon, it would be too late. If I could will myself to lactate and fortify them even for an hour, I would.

I closed my eyes. My lungs ached so I had to bypass the three deep breaths but was still able to relax my body to the consistency of Jell-O on a stick. I fell quickly and woefully into my Alpha level:

My quiet place is on the lapping shores of a desert island. My statuesque frame is draped in a clinging white see-through gossamer house dress, my short blond pixie hairdo highlighting my equally pixie-ish features. I'm looking absolutely fabulous. Technically, I am a grandmother but frankly, everyone finds it hard to believe. I radiate youth and health, have an inquisitive mind and endless energy. A herd of enamored children are lounging around my golden chaise longue listening intently to my exciting true life adventures which I enjoy sharing with them. All of the extremely well behaved tykes refer to me as either Ni-Ni, Darra, or Mrs. van Zandt. They are devoted to me. I am their favorite grandperson. It is their greatest pleasure to wait on me hand and foot—bringing me my silver sandals, mixing up a batch of onion dip or the occasional platter of Nachos Supremo with fresh guac. And the boy, the one I call Jack—he already mixes a mean Cuba Libre—never forgetting to rub the rim of the frosted glass with a lime wedge. I allow the youngest to apply lipstick to my full mouth and blush my cheeks. Not that I need it. My cheeks are naturally rosy. Our island is a land of plenty. There are miles of coconut trees, hundreds of goats and cows always eager to be milked and groves of mango, papaya, avocado and banana trees. Our trusty handyman is a big, blond behemoth crumpet with muscles bulging out from every limb attached to his ripply suntanned torso, with a matching buttocks barely covered by a clinging white see-through house thong. He is busy building an addition to our already luxurious six bedroom split-level hut. Today I believe he is adding another walk-in closet to our master bedroom. We could go back to civilization anytime we wanted to on one of the three fine sailing ships our handyman has crafted. And one day we will. But not now. Not yet. Right now our life is too wonderful to change a thing. We are contented and feel safe. We...

The shock of the boat tilting violently to the left brought me quickly out of my Alpha Level of consciousness and into the real world. The familiar hand attempting to pull its owner aboard was causing the boat to almost capsize. I screamed and fell on top of the basket leaning back as far as I could to bring the boat back right. A pin striped leg lunged over and on to the boat with a sickening grunt to bring Mabouk back in our lives. Again. The flesh on his face was hanging in rubbery raspberry red shreds and his 200 plus head hairs had been singed away along with his eyebrows and eyelashes. He looked like a premenstrual pit bull. He growled at me and without much strain wrestled away one of the two oars I had immediately grabbed to use as weapons. We were both standing. Not a good idea in a dingy. We fenced back and forth, the boat tipping precariously with each swipe of the oar. I was not going to give up after having gone so far. He barked at me again and this time I surprised him—as well as myself, by roaring back, a wild look in my eyes like a lioness protecting her cubs. I put every *nth* of strength I had left and swung the oar at him with all my might, just as he was swinging at me.

I think I heard a crack, but then that was it. Nothing. That was it for me. Curtains.

There was a light. THE light. That warm white light I've heard so much about when one is about to "go over to the other side". It was bright like a spotlight but it was also in a tunnel and I had this uncontrollable urge to follow it. Drawn to the end of the tunnel, I couldn't get there fast enough. I ran. When I reached the end, I saw my grandma, Elsie Mabel, young and beautiful, followed by a flock of devoted children. Then his face appeared before me. Philippe. He was dressed in white and stood in the center of an even brighter crown of light. His hand reached out to me but I wasn't sure if I should take it or not. I was deeply tempted because he looked like a babe, as usual. But if I take his hand, does that mean that's it? I. T.? Like I'll never see my family again? I wanted to think about it for a minute. I don't do fast decisions—but his hand reached for me with even more force. Hey, I thought this was *my* choice? I thought I could make the ultimate final decision on if I'm ready to "go over" or not. The hand yanked harder but instead of going over, I was being pulled out of the ocean by a French Police helicopter. Philippe was holding tight to both of my hands as we straddled the basket attached to the rescue line swinging from the chopper. Once we were aboard, the powerful spotlight continued to scan the sea and wreckage for more survivors, but it was obvious that we were the only lucky ones.

We were finally safe. But life as I once knew it would never be the same. I knew that. It was precisely what I asked for, was it not? A taste of Life. I was cognizant of where I was but could not react—to speak—to cry—to reach out for Philippe, this fair haired angel sent down to protect me through this walk on the wild side of life—A Kiss of Life. He was speaking softly in my ear but I couldn't hear a damn thing except the thwacking of the helicopter blade which was adding to my throbbing headache with each revolution.

By the time we touched down on the landing pad at the Air France Tower in Paris, the five babes had been fed, changed and bundled up snugly thanks to the La Croix Rouge nurse that Philippe had quickly organized to accompany the search party. They were all fine. Philippe had a slight concussion as a result of the struggle with Mabouk when he hit his head on his fall into the water near the harbor. Luckily, Capt. Gaudette had just reassembled his squad to follow us out to sea when Philippe washed up to the dock. The fiery glow of the Golden Empress on the horizon led them like a beacon in the night to rescue us.

If it hadn't been for all the loose ends, like five orphans and the mute and traumatized young redheaded girl, I would say everything had worked out swell. Antoine was back home with his Marie-Louise and Angelique, and with very minimal pressure applied, Hank and the doc had spilled the beans in intricate detail about the entire baby selling operation, implicating reps in Italy, Germany and my own adopted country, Holland! The French Coast Guard's second search for survivors of the Golden Empress came up with zero, so we had to assume that Mabouk, Malika, Jacques and Cook had finally received their just reward and were pushing up seaweed daisies somewhere at the bottom of the blue Mediterranean.

It was 5:00 A.M. Paris was still asleep. I dozed on Philippe's shoulder on the way to the hospital where I had a quick going over. I had first degree burns on my feet, smoke inhalation and a goose bump on my noggin, but nothing serious enough to keep me from going home today. I ached to be back in Bozum, to play Barbies with Christina, to see Soul Mate, to leave a recorded message on Christian's answer machine in California.

The Etoile du Nord was leaving at 11:00 A.M. I had six hours to recuperate and say my good-byes. My first stop was the hotel to pick up my things. Philippe pulled up on the curb and came with me. I had to pound on the outside door for ten minutes until I finally roused Marcel from his current wet dream.

147

Oui, qu 'est que vous voulez? he said with goo in his eyes and absolutely no recognition of the face of this guest—a regular guest—probably the only guest cheap enough to stay here.

Bun-jur, Marcel. It's me, Darra van Zandt. I'm in Room 13, third floor, remember? I'm checking out.

He handed me the key and snoozed off in a standing position.

Philippe waited for me in reception. I was too embarrassed to let him see how low I often stoop to save a few francs on a hotel room so I firmly refused his offer to help me gather the few items I had left scattered around the room. I stuffed the smelly black Levi's down to the bottom of my bag hoping the still ripe odor would not permeate the cotton sack. As I left the room, I got a flash of myself in the warped mirror on the wall and cried all the way down to reception.

Philippe immediately sensed something wrong. Isn't that just him? *What is it, Darra? You have been so brave, so strong through all of this. What is it? Is it the children? What is it? Please tell me,* my darling.

He didn't really say "my darling"—wishful thinking just added it.

Wahhhh haaahhhh, I wailed like I Love Lucy. *It's...It's....It's meeeeeee, Look at meeeeee......*

You? But you are beautiful. Very beautiful. Darra, do you have any idea how heroic you are? It was you, Darra. All you. I was just there to protect....uhmmm, help you, that's all. Please try to see yourself as the beautiful being I see before me.

His tender words soothed me and I calmed down.

Marcel was asleep on the black, fake fur divan behind the reception desk. He slept through the racket of my emotional collapse in the lobby so I didn't bother to wake him up to pay my room tab. I left the money on the counter and we left.

148

The Trudeau's had been calling the Paris Police station all night. Philippe drove me there next. Antoine came to the door in a red silk robe and black suede slippers with gold A.T.'s embroidered on the front. He was none the worse for wear, this guy—a truly remarkable comeback. He looked like he should have looked all along. He must have taken a nice long bath in that black marble bathtub and rejuvenated himself with all sorts of expensive bath beads and lotions. Marie-Louise was also looking like she was ready to promenade down a catwalk, dressed in a pale blue satin peignoir, highheeled backless satin slippers with puff balls accentuating every step. The blue complimented her flowing blond tresses.

Tresses. Speaking of which. What about my tresses? I have no bangs, no sides and enough in the back to make a pencil thin ponytail.

Both Marie-Louise and Antoine drew me into their arms and hugged me so tight I thought I was gonna throw up. My lungs were still sore and Antoine stepped on my bandaged right foot during his sincere show of appreciation.

Yeowwww, I tried to stifle but couldn't. *Hi, you guys. You all right? You look grreat, really.* I pulled away. I also didn't want to frump them up.

Oh, oui, Darra. Everyzhing iz merveilleux for uz today. Today iz ze birzday of our daughter and we are togethzer. You give uz a pricelez cadeau. Merci, merci, Darra.

Well, I'm so happy to see you all together again. I had to see it with my own eyes before I left Paris.

Darra, mon ami, said my new best friend, Marie-Louise. *You muzt allow me to take care of you now. Zit here. Pleazah. I will be right back.*

I didn't have the strength to argue. Antoine poured us all a large café au lait and I listened as Philippe took the police report. Antoine cleansed his soul, pouring out everything he knew including his share of the blame. He felt responsible for keeping Mabouk in business for the last few years by providing the documents and consequently destroying the lives of young girls, while he enjoyed his own fatherhood.

Marie-Louise came back into the living room and sat next to her husband on the large white ottoman. She gave me a sly smile.

What the? I thought.

Antoine went on…

We…Marie-Louizah and I, we feel zhere iz zo much we want to do to make up for zhese children and zheir zuffering. We 'ave dizcuzzed and we know zhat ze only way to make right iz to take full rezponzibility of zhese children. We like to leave Pariz and live in our country home wiz Angelique and all five bébéz and alzo ze young girl tortured zo brutally on ze boat. She can be wiz her child and alzo help us wiz ze othzerz. Of courze we will 'have ze othzer help alzo. We will do whatever iz necezzary for making ziz a pozzibility to come true. I will cooperate wiz you, Inspector Clement, to turn myzelf into ze authorities for my involvement but we will prove to ze magistrate our zincere to make amendz.

Philippe listened intently but I could see that he was doubtful as to whether the law would be so lenient on an accomplice to such a heinous crime. Perhaps he could be instrumental in the apprehension of the rest of the members of the organization—perhaps to testify against them, Trudeau bargained. It was worth a try, said Philippe and continued taking his report.

Nineteen

*D*ing Dong. Chanel calling. Marie-Louise opened the front door to let in a small army of repair people. Etienne was already sizing up my recent haircut, Monique was whipping up cleansing grains as she walked through to the bathroom, and a little man with a tape measure around his neck, a mouthful of tailoring pins and a large box under one arm, did circles around me going, *uh hmm, uh hmmm.*

It was 7:30 AM. They whisked me away to the Trudeau's palatial bathroom and got started. Monique loofahed layers of soot, dirt and age off my face and body, masked me in green mud and had me simmer for a half hour in a decadent almond milk bath, my bandaged feet hanging over the side of the tub. Unsophisticated pores throughout my body screamed, *Agghhhh, what gives? What's with the dairy products?*

With my new skin properly nourished, tingling and "resting," Etienne took over to give me a new hairdo—the only one possible with all the clumps of hair chopped off courtesy of little Angelique—a pixie! I looked—you got it—absolutely fabulous! All of the blond frosting had been snipped off by the little miss, so he applied a terrific ultra-light color over my whole head. Except for the age, face and figure, I looked like very much like that famous model, Linda Evangelista, in *her* blond pixie phase.

Monique's turn again. She treated my face as if it were a priceless Ming vase, her fingers moving like butterfly wings against my new visage. I dotted my mole myself. For the first time in a long time I didn't feel like an old gray moth.

By the time they were both through with me, coiffure and maquillage complete, I was feeling no more pain. Marie-Louise had laid out a sexy pair of black lacy briefs, underwire bra and silky teddy on the bed. I pushed my white Hanes For Her down to the bottom of my quilted duffel bag where they belonged next to my jeans, and was about to slip on my new lingerie when I spied that stupid weigh scale in the bathroom just calling my name.

I only did it because I knew I couldn't have put on any weight, what with the events of the last few days, so I boldly stepped up, watched the red lights tease me til they stopped on 137.5! Can today get any better? I had lost almost six pounds in five days. I coughed in sync with the beeps as I got off, and proudly slipped on my new undies. I hunted through my bag to find something decent to wear on the train but the only possibility was the Chanel T-shirt and black leggings that I had left here when I went off to meet Mabouk. Everything else in the bag stunk.

At that moment, little Monsieur Croteau barged in the room, lassoed me in with his black and gold tape measure and in fifteen seconds— before I had a chance to be modest, he had all he needed.

Pas de problème, he said. *Vous etes tres belle, Madame. Tres belle.*

Attendez ici. Then he left the room.

I waited for ten minutes but I was getting nervous about the time; afraid I'd miss my train, so I started to get dressed in my Batman outfit.

Non, non, non, Madame, Monsieur Croteau called out from the doorway just in the knick of time. *C'est pour vous*…as he held up the new suit for me. Chanel. Pink. Pink with black trim just like the other one. Chains. Lots of gold chains. Black handbag. Chains. Lots of gold chains. Shoes. Black flats with pink trim. One size larger so my bandages would squeeze in.

Etienne and Monique gave me finishing touches, reminding me to keep my shoulders back, head up as I entered the Trudeau living room runway looking like the last model of a successful show. You know, the special one, the bride—the one who always gets to wear the wedding dress.

Antoine and Marie-Louise *oohed* and *ahhed* me but my eyes were on Philippe, whose eyes were on me. We were stuck together…eyewise.

Darra, you look marvelous, said he. *Are you feeling better now?* I could tell he was a little bit flustered and had to make small talk to downplay the electricity generating between us right in front of the Trudeau's.

Just then, Angelique woke up and called from the nursery so both understandably overprotective parents ran to comfort her.

That left us alone.

Darra.

Philippe.

We spoke at the same time.

You go first, I said.

No, no, you go first, he insisted.

No, really. I can't even remember what I was gonna say anyway. Go ahead, Philippe. You first.

Okay. Here goes. Darra, there's something I must tell you and I don't want you to be shocked when I say this...

Of course not, Philippe. Nothing you say can shock me, sweetheart. No, I didn't really say "sweetheart"...

Well, you know when I first laid eyes on you in the café, I...

Pring, pring. Telephone.

Allo, oui. Oui, c'est la familie Trudeau. Avec qui est ce que je parle? Marie-Louise ran into the living room to catch it on the second ring.

Oui, oui, un instant. Darra, itz for you. Itz your 'uzband.

My feet walked over to the phone without me. When I finally caught up I said, *Hello? Oh, hi, honeeee. Where in the world are you calling from and how did you know where to reach me? Are you still in Texas? Oh...oh, really? Oh. What a nice surprise. That's grreeeat. So you're home early. Terrific.*

Me? Oh, well I'm sure Marielle told you about my Aunt Trudy. You remember I told you I had an Aunt Trudy? Yeah, my dear old Auntie. Such a shame. She's always been so full of life. Anyway, I'll give you the details when I get home. Other than that? Oh, not much really. Just a bit of shopping and a visit to the beauty parlor. I also met a couple of nice people here and I'm just saying my good-byes before I catch the 11:00 o'clock train to Amsterdam. How marvey that you're home early, sweet patootie. Can't wait to see you. And Christina? Is she okay? Can I talk to her? Oh, okay, sure I understand. Tell her I can't wait to see her tonight. Oh, wait a minute, sweets. Did Christian happen to call by any chance? He did? Is he gonna call back? Is he home? Did he tell you where I could reach him? To speak to him— live? Yeah, okay, I got it. Yup. I know he's busy. I know. Hey, listen, I'll see you tonight, okay? Yeah, I will. I promise. See you. Bye.

All the while I was talking to Soul Mate, Philippe was burying himself in his police report but I could sense him listening to my telephone conversation and even more, analyzing its content.

I hope you do not mind zhat I give your bébézitter ziz telephone number, Darra, but yezterday when you left to meet Mabouk and left your clothez and identification here, I felt I should call your home to leave ze mezzage for you. Did I ze wrong zing? You are not angry?

No, no, Marie-Louise. It's all right. I was going to also call but with all that's gone on time just ran away from me. No, really, thank you for thinking of it. Well, I guess it's time I left for Gare du Nord. May I call a taxi, Antoine?

Of course not, Darra. Philippe protested. *I'll take you to the train. Don't be ridiculous. My car is just outside.*

The grateful couple hugged me tight, did the three kisses on the cheek thing and we all promised to keep in touch forever.

I left the penthouse with Philippe—our business still unfinished.

Twenty

Gare du Nord was crowded at this time of day so Philippe left his official car on the curb with the blue light flashing. We stopped at the first souvenir kiosk, where I picked out a jeweled bracelet with a miniature Eiffel tower dangling from it for Christina, then found the departure track, Voie 11, for the Etoile du Nord to Amsterdam, via Brussels. The First Class dining room was the second to the last car. My scorched feet were beginning to ache with every step so I had to hold on to Philippe's arm to relieve some of the pressure from my new shoes. All right, so it was a good excuse. With only five minutes left for us to profess our undying love for each other and to hopefully make a date to meet at the top of the Eiffel tower on New Year's Eve five years from today, we had to work fast. He's too shy to initiate, I knew that. I gotta say something now, before it's too late. This is crazy, I said to myself. Just as I was about to take the lead, we reached the dining car and he lifted me up the two steps to the doorway landing. I told him to wait a sec and hastily went to the restaurant car, put my things on an empty seat next to a table for four already occupied by two women.

He was still waiting, God love him.

It was 10:59. The train would be pulling out of the station any second. It felt like it was already in motion and I still didn't get to tell Philippe how I felt about him. And he me. Our last chance.

Suddenly I was Loretta Young saying farewell to Farley Granger:

It is midnight. The train platform is shrouded in fog. A lonely lantern flickers in the distance. Ten fingertips make frantic love as they separate for the last time…the conductor's whistle ends what never was, what could have been…

I was moving. Philippe walked along side of the train and I could swear his eyes were moist when he said, *Hey, kid. We're a good team, aren't we? You take good care of yourself, ya hear?*

I will, don't worry. Hey, Philippe, what were you about to tell me back at the Trudeau's, before the phone rang?

Uh. Oh, it wasn't anything really. It's just that…

Tooooooottttttooooot. Train whistle.

*What did you say? I didn't hear yoouuuu…*I yelled back trying not to sound so desperate.

He was a hundred yards and a million miles behind me now. I tried to read his lips but could only see that they were moving.

I took a chance. *I love you toooooooo…*

I watched him as he became smaller and my heart grew heavier. Tears clouded by vision. I had to keep him in sight to hold on to him for as long as possible, if not forever. Then. Then he disappeared in a brillant flash of light at the exact moment I felt an incredibly wonderful wave of warmth flow through my body. I was numb. But not a bad numb.

Before joining the dining room I thought I'd make a stop to the W.C. to be alone for a few minutes. I could cry in here. The rattle of the toilet fixtures and clacking of the Etoile du Nord leaving the train yard could drown out what would ordinarily come next. I looked at myself in the oblong mirror ready to let the waterworks go, but I didn't have to cry. I was composed. And I wasn't off on one of my relaxation therapy exercises either. This was real life. The Beta level. I loved myself "unconditionally". And I looked great.

My mirror, my friend.

I took my place next to the window at the table with the two women, both American, and turned my head away from them....to "look at the scenery". Although I felt rather good, I wasn't ready to indulge in any superficial chit chat.

When the waiter came back with my small order of a plate of cheese, some French bread and a glass of Bordeaux, I didn't let his display of annoyance affect me and nibbled and sipped without much zesto. I didn't really have much enthusiasm to eavesdrop either—a favorite family pastime, but sitting at the same table, for goodness sake, made it inevitable:

Tiffany, you know what? you really have to come to make a decision with this whole Todd what's-his-face relationship. I mean, if you don't empower yourself now, girlfriend, you will be in denial for the rest of your life. First, you must get involved with a 12 step program to learn how to cope with your dysfunctional family experience and even, yes even become enriched by it. You must get in touch with your inner-child if you are ever to become whole again. To be one with the universe. No one wants or asks to be a co-dependent. It just happens. Shit happens. Second child syndrome. What can I say? You didn't ask to be "second child," did you? Don't beat yourself up about it. Don't be so hard on yourself. Remember that guy, Blake Bledstone? Well, I tell ya, my experience with Blake Bledstone brought out the egg-zact same feelings surfacing with you now. I know. Don't tell me, honey. Been there. Done that. If I hadn't found my support group when I did, I'd be in big trouble today. Sure, I didn't think I needed it either until my family and truest friends intervened and made me see my problem. I was blocking. I was blocking. And you know what? Today I am healthy and you, my dear friend, can be healthy too, as soon as you can turn your negative energy into positive energy...

I looked around to see if there might be an available space at another table. There wasn't. I couldn't bear the thought of listening to their psychological mumbo jumbo for the next three hours. I felt a strong urge to "intervene" and offer my own gratis advice to Tiffany and it would even take less than one minute. One sentence really: Dump the jerk and get a life. Period. Next!

However, I could tell that the dime store shrink across from me was enjoying hearing herself advise her friend-patient, who looked like her brain was made out of very porous sponge matter, so I found it in my gentle heart not to interrupt. She was in complete control, this counselor. She looked rather harmless. A cute dark cropped layered cut—we used to call it an "artichoke" back in the sixties—a style I, myself, have always fancied, and a simple statement beige gabardine suit. It matched up with a cream silk blouse, expensive faux jewelry and well-groomed American hands.

I unconsciously balled my fists together and put them on my lap— there wasn't much the Chanel team could do with my paws in such a short time. Anyway, I think she was what they call these days, a "nurturer" or a "guider". Or is it a buttinski? Or, is it a smart ass who likes to hear her own voice?

Tiffany, the patient, had straight black hair, big bulging brown eyes, a nondescript nose and a mouth that hung open in perpetual awe. And, like I said, absorbent gray matter between her ears. She was also chicly dressed in a gray wool power suit, no accessories.

Smart. The clothes, that is, not them. I wondered how in the heck these gals had made it so far up their corporate ladders with so many, many, many problems and hang-ups. I mean they appeared to be successful businesswomen. They were definitely not tourists but more likely on business in Europe with expense accounts since they weren't at all shocked, as I always am, when they read the menu. They went all out, as one would if one were on an expense account: Their appetizer was a rip off three scrawny baby shrimp on a bed of lettuce—more like four spinach leaves organized in a semi-circle, and dotted, and I mean dotted, with a dot of caviar. Six eggs max.

The starter course passed without incident, but when the main course arrived, they got into the real American take-back mode, making me instantly homesick for my homeland:

Excuse me. Ex-cuse me, garsohn, said the assertive shrink to the waiter. *Excuse me, I hate to say this but you know what? I'm afraid I can't eat this meat so rare. Could you please take it back and have it cooked for just two or three minutes, no more, so it is more pinkish colored, not so red?* She made a squinched up face when she said "red". *And I don't mean well done, please. If it comes back well done, then I'm sorry but I'll have to have you take it back again because I also cannot eat well-done meat. Oh, and by the way, this time, could you ask the chef to not use any butter or oil unless it is canola or olive, and even then, use it sparingly, please. Thank you. Oh, and excuse me*, she called out again as he walked away. *Excuse me. I'm sorry to bother you again, but I thought I asked for the boiled potatoes and these look like they might have been fried in animal fat and I don't eat animal fat. I'm sorry but could you please bring back boiled potatoes when you return my steak? Thanks so much. I'm sorry to be such a bother but I really can't eat it any other way. Is yours okay, Tiff?*

The waiter heard her inquire about her friend's meal but he walked away without waiting for a response, thus, in a sense walking all over the many times walked over already, "Tiff". He obviously didn't give a hoot about how "Tiff's" meal scored, or what is more important, how it made her "feel".

W-el-ll, I guess so, she limply murmured. *I haven't tried the vegetables yet. I was hoping they'd have fish or chicken on the menu. This is the second time this month I'm eating meat and I can really feel it. It gives me that sluggish, low energy feeling. Oh well, what can you do? We're here. We have to rough it. We'll be going home in a few days and I personally can't wait. Can you be-lieve how the people live in these countries? I mean did you see the size of the bathroom in the hotel? Un-bu-liev-a-bul. Anyway...* going back to her plate, separating and flipping around the limp veggies with her fork, *I guessss mine is o-kahyee.*

I was finished with my camembert and gruyere and was feeling a little ornery so I decided to give them another way to "channel their anger". I pulled out my pack of Marlboros and asked the shrink if she had a light. Well, you might have thought I had asked if it would be all right if I killed her cat.

After my table mates made a big stink about my smoking, I snubbed out the butt halfway to leave an annoying trail of old smoke on the table forcing one of them to *eewww* touch "it" if they wanted to kill it. I paid the bill, took my glass of wine and got up to hunt out another available seat. The handy extra set of eyes in the back of my head and the radar hearing that God gave me to observe people looking and talking maliciously about me could easily detect the two women checking me out from head to toe and commenting on my dirty habit as I confidently strolled out of the car. I found an empty compartment two cars down but as soon as I was alone and had closed the curtains, my cocky façade came tumbling down and I felt as though I might have another little breakdown to round out the weekend. Luckily, I was diverted by the reflection of my new look in the compartment window. God, I looked good. I turned this way and that—even danced around a little until the conductor caught me, wouldn'tcha know.

We got closer to Amsterdam and I was pleasantly surprised to find myself very anxious to see Soul Mate and Christina. And to call Christian in California. But I could not discount the fact that this getaway weekend churned up a desire to live my life the way I wanted to—not the way I was expected to live it. Philippe will always hold a very special place in my heart, as will the Trudeau's, the babies and their unlucky mothers. Ironically, it was through their misfortune that I was able to accept that I, too, am maternal and should not "be so hard on myself"….

It was raining when I stepped off the train in Bozum. I had to drag my quilted duffel bag the half block to my house from the station. As I turned the corner to my street, I could I see the lights of my little house beckoning me home—Soul Mate was standing in the doorway with Christina in his arms. She wiggled away from her father and ran to meet me, a present clutched in her hand. She made it at school. It was a hand mirror made out of purple construction paper, a white lace cake doily and a tin can lid with a face painted in the reflection…the face of her mother: a big red smile above what looked like a double chin, green eyes, thin eyebrows and a mole above the upper lip. Above the orange head of hair detailed with black roots, was written in gold letters:

"Mirror, mirror on the wall,

Who's the most beautiful mama of them all? You".

As I took Christina's hand and walked toward Soul Mate, I realized I was turning another corner in my life.

Dear Lord, thanks *soooo* much for keeping me safe all weekend. You really know how to show a girl a good time.

The check is in the mail, Sir.

www.ingramcontent.com/pod-product-compliance
Lightning Source LLC
Chambersburg PA
CBHW020430290526
45785CB00002B/781